Frederick Manson Bailey

The Fern World of Australia

With homes of the Queensland species

Frederick Manson Bailey

The Fern World of Australia
With homes of the Queensland species

ISBN/EAN: 9783337319380

Printed in Europe, USA, Canada, Australia, Japan

Cover: Foto ©Andreas Hilbeck / pixelio.de

More available books at **www.hansebooks.com**

The Fern World of Australia

BY

FRED. MANSON BAILEY

Price

GORDON & GOTCH
BRISBANE
SYDNEY. MELBOURNE. & LONDON

Be
de
th
of

Gr
Co

out
: is
Tea

ipal
A N

LOVE & COMPANY,
TEA IMPORTERS, Eastern & Commission Merchants,
EDWARD STREET, BRISBANE.
And at 79 York Street, Sydney.

 **FIRST PRIZE.**

W. EDDS,

PRIZE BUGGY BUILDER,

AUSTRALIAN COACH FACTORY, ALBERT STREET,

And Melbourne Coach Works,

CORNER OF CHARLOTTE STREET,
BRISBANE.

Buggies Made to Order.

BY APPOINTMENT
TO HIS

EXCELLENCY THE
GOVERNOR.

MR. D. R. EDEN,

SURGEON DENTIST,

QUEEN STREET,

BRISBANE.

THE

FERN WORLD

OF

AUSTRALIA,

WITH

HOMES OF THE QUEENSLAND SPECIES,

NEW YORK
BOTANICAL
BY GARDEN

FREDK. MANSON BAILEY, F.L.S.

Corr. Mem. Royal Society, Tasmania; Corr. Mem. Royal Society,
Victoria; Corr. Mem. Royal Society, South Australia; Corr. Mem. Linnean
Society, N. S. Wales; Hon. Mem. Gard. Society, Adelaide; Hon. Mem.
Queensland Philosophical Society, &c.

WITH PLATES ILLUSTRATING FERN TRIBES.

"For many years it has been one of my constant regrets that no school-
master of mine had a knowledge of natural history, so far, at least as to
have taught me the grasses that grow by the wayside, the little winged or
wingless neighbours that are continually meeting me with a salutation
that I cannot answer as things are."—CARLYLE.

BRISBANE:
PUBLISHED BY GORDON AND GOTCH,
BRISBANE, SYDNEY, MELBOURNE, AND LONDON

1881.

ADVERTISEMENT.

In this work there is a Glossary of Terms used in the description of Ferns, while the local name as well as the derivation of the botanical name is always given.

At the end there is a copious and comprehensive Index, which contains all the synonyms under which each species has been published in other works.

TO

THE REV. J. E. TENISON-WOODS, F.G.S., L.S., &c., &c.

PRESIDENT OF THE LINNÆAN SOCIETY OF N. S. WALES.

THIS LITTLE WORK

IS MOST RESPECTFULLY DEDICATED IN TOKEN

OF THE GREAT HELP HE HAS RENDERED

TO SCIENCE IN AUSTRALIA

AND PERSONAL KINDNESS AND ASSISTANCE

TO HIS

OBLIGED AND OBEDIENT

SERVANT,

THE AUTHOR.

CONTENTS.

	PAGE
I.—Introduction including guide to Fern study	1
II.—Remarks on collecting and cultivation	4
III.—Queensland species arranged in groups	6
Group I. Climbing ferns.	6
,, II. Creekside ferns.	7
,, III. Epiphytal ferns.	8
,, IV. Forest ferns.	9
,, V. Rock ferns.	11
,, VI. Scrub ferns.	14
,, VII. Swamp ferns.	16
,, VIII. Tree ferns.	17
IV.—Australian Ferns systematically arranged in the following six tribes:—	19
Tribe I. Ophioglosseæ.	19
,, II. Marattieæ.	21
,, III. Osmundeæ.	24
,, IV. Hymenophylleæ.	27
,, V. Cyatheeæ.	31
,, VI. Polypodieæ.	35
V.—A short glossary	81
VI.—List of authorities for generic and specific names ...	84
VII.—Index of genera, species, and synonyms, to which is added the local name, or meaning of name used. ...	86
Addenda—containing the Australian Lycopods. ...	76

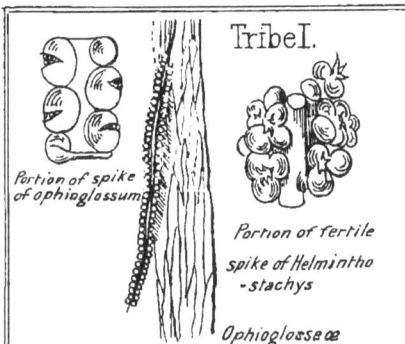

Portion of spike
of ophioglossum

Tribe I.

Portion of fertile
spike of Helmintho
-stachys

Ophioglosseæ

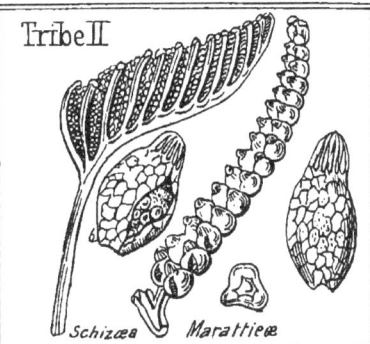

Tribe II

Schizæa *Marattieæ*

Tribe III

Osmundeæ

Gleichenia *Todea*

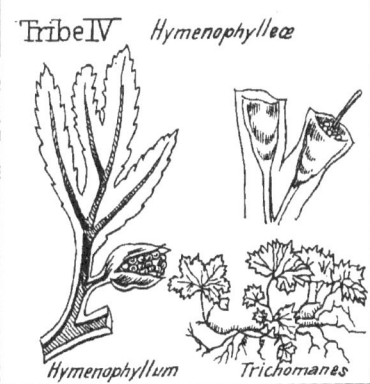

Tribe IV *Hymenophylleæ*

Hymenophyllum *Trichomanes*

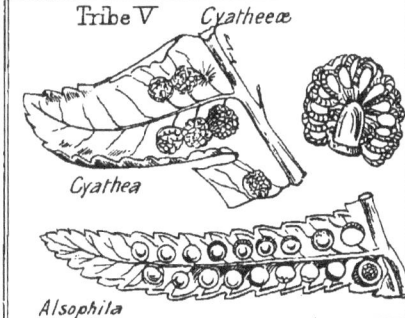

Tribe V *Cyatheeæ*

Cyathea

Alsophila

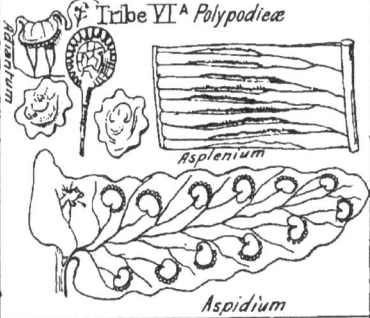

Tribe VI ᴬ *Polypodieæ*

Adiantum

Asplenium

Aspidium

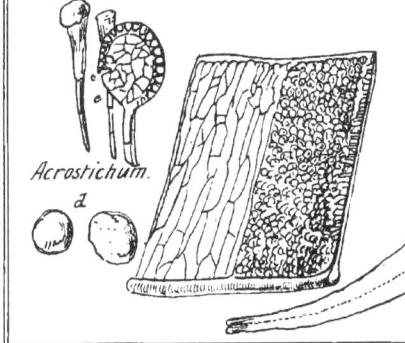

Tribe VI ᴮ *Polypodieæ*

Acrostichum.
d

Polypodium

LYCOPODIACEÆ

Lycopodium

Selaginella

Tmesipteris

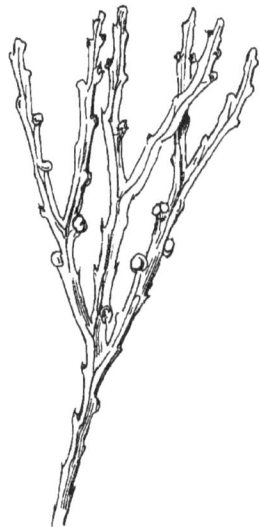

Psilotum

INDEX
OF
ENGLISH NAMES.

	Page.
Adder's-tongue	19
Bat's-wing Fern	46
Bird's-nest Fern	52
Black Tree Fern of New Zealand	33
Bladder Fern	58
Blanket Fern	71
Bracken Fern	46
Braid Fern	25
Bristle Fern	27
Caraway-seed Fern	56
Common Bracken	46
Curly Fern	43
Deer's-tongue	72
Ear Fern	45
Elk's-horn Fern	74
English Maiden-hair	41
Fan Fern	26
Fan-shaped Spleenwort	53
Film Fern	30
Golden Swamp Fern	73
Grape Fern	20
Grass-leaved Fern	38
Hare's-foot Fern	37
Jersey Fern	71
Lady Fern	60
Maiden-hair Fern	41
Maiden-hair Spleenwort	53
Meadow-rue Water Fern	24
Moonwort	20
Mountain Bracken	37
Parasol Fern	25
Pickled Cabbage Fern	49
Potatoe Fern	24
Prickly Fern	51
Prickly-tree Fern	34
Ribbon Fern	20
Rough-stalked Maiden-hair	42
Shield Fern	58
Shiny Fern	64
Small Maiden-hair	42
Snake's-tongue	21
Spleenwort Fern	52
Stag's-horn	74
Tall Maiden-hair Fern	42
Woolly-tree Fern	35

PREFACE.

FERNS are perhaps the most beautiful order in the whole range of the Vegetable Kingdom; they have at all times been favorites with the lovers of the beautiful. Other orders of plants have been extolled for a time, after which they have been placed on one side and forgotten. But with the fern, one is never weary; there is a peculiar fascination about these lovely forms of vegetation. They are always welcome, and draw forth our admiration, whether we see them covering the damp or dry rock, clothing the stems of our gigantic scrub trees, or pendant from their huge forks. They are eagerly sought after by young and old—by some for the gratification of the present moment, by others for cultivation about their homes, or for the purpose of decoration. Indeed, so attractive are these beauties of Flora's Kingdom, that it is almost impossible to find a house where they are not to be met with either living or dead. Thus it may be easily inferred that a knowledge of their nomenclature, classification, and local habitat, would be acceptable; and it is with such an idea that this little work is offered to the public. Since the publication of the author's former work on the Queensland Ferns, the 7th Volume of Bentham and Mueller's elaborate work "The FLORA AUSTRALIENSIS" has been issued containing the ferns. It has been deemed, therefore, advisable to follow the classification there adopted in the present work, thus keeping so far as possible from a confusion of nomenclature.

Another advantage, it is hoped, will be found in the work containing all the ferns at present known to inhabit Australia and Tasmania, thus rendering it equally useful in each of the colonies. The expediency of this course will be obvious when it is pointed out that two-fourths of the kinds met with in Australia are found in Queensland, conjointly with one or other of the other colonies. One-fourth in Queensland, but not in adjoining colonies, leaving only one-fourth of the whole as ing to the other colonies without Queensland. It is worthy also to remark that the indigenous ferns of Queensland equal in number those of the Islands of New Zealand, and are three times the number of those of Great Britain.

The author cannot conclude these prefatory remarks without acknowledging his indebtedness to the learned works of Robert Brown, Bentham, Mueller, Hooker, Smith, Moore, &c., &c.; and would also express his sincere thanks to the many friends from whom he has received assistance, specially, Sir Ferd. von Mueller, of Melbourne ; the Rev. J. E. Tenison-Woods, Dr. Chas. Prentice, Brisbane; Dr. Rich. Schomburgk, of Adelaide ; Chas. Moore, Esq., of Sydney; Dr. Bancroft, Brisbane ; L. A. Bernays, Esq., Brisbane; all of whom are indefatigable workers in the cause of science. Also to Miss F. M. Campbell, of Gippsland ; and Mrs. A. Archer, of Brisbane, for information regarding habitat and specimens of rare species.

INTRODUCTION.

" I cannot but think the very complacency and satisfaction which a man
   takes in the works of Nature to be a laudable if not virtuous habit of
   mind."—*Addison*.

In writing or speaking about any portion of the vast flora of
Australia, one labours under many disadvantages, unknown to those
who write about the plants of countries which have been longer
known. One great drawback is the want of local or native names.
It may be safely said that no other country is so badly off in this
respect. In all other parts of the world the botanist can fall back
on the native name, but in Australia that is quite impossible, the
character of the natives and the extent of territory entirely pre-
vent it.

In the present work great pains and care have been taken to add
as many local names as possible, but as many of our ferns are as
yet imperfectly known to the botanist, it cannot be expected that
such should possess local names, though doubtless as these are
received from time to time into cultivation, each will receive one.

In studying these beautiful plants, two courses are open to the
student ; the one by collecting living plants and cultivating them
in suitable situations, whereby their habits and developement could
be more carefully observed : the other by forming what is termed
an herbarium of well selected specimens, and it must be borne in
mind that for this purpose portions of each part of the plant should
be collected, and should the species produce fronds of various shapes
each form should be preserved, but most particularly the soriferous
or fruit bearing fronds.

It may be well before proceeding to the enumeration of our species,
to give some few notes on the structure of a fern, to prepare the
student for that part of the work wherein ferns are described.

The leaves, or more correctly speaking branches of a fern are
termed *fronds*, on some of these will be observed, by paying a little
attention, dust-like patches which are situated either on the back or
edge of these fronds, these patches or heaps which are called *sori*,
are sometimes covered by a thin skin, and consist of numerous one-
celled bladders. In the largest tribe these bladders are girt
longitudinally by a jointed ring which at maturity contracts and
thus ruptures the bladder, and allows the escapement of the contained
spores which are individually invisible to the unassisted eye.

With the exception of one tribe the leaves (fronds) are, while
young, rolled inwards (circinate) like a crosier,

The roots are all fibrous and usually densely covered with soft
close hairs mostly of a rusty colour.

B

The thick hard part, from which spring the fronds, is the stem, and is mostly called in works on ferns the *Rhizome* or rootstock ; sometimes this stem will be found creeping over rocks or trees, at other times it will be found some distance below the surface of the earth. In creeping or climbing kinds the growing part will always be found in advance of the leaves (fronds), the more distant of which are the most likely to be fertile, that is to say bearing *sori*, or seed patches.

In the short tufted form of stem, the leaves are developed around the growing point, the bases of the older leaves helping to form its trunk ; these stems are sometimes reclining, but in what are called tree ferns they become trunk-like. In one tribe they are in the form of a large fleshy globose mass of several hundredweight.

The leaves or fronds of ferns are of two parts. The stalk or *stipes*, that is the portion from the rootstock or rhizome, to the blade or ramified part. These *stipites* or stalks are either adherent to the rootstock, or at or near will be formed a joint or articulation, in which case the frond will be said to be articulated to the rootstock, this structure is often carried out throughout every division of the frond, and in such cases much care is required in preparing herbarium specimens. The continuation of the stalk through the leafy portion of the frond, when the latter is divided into leaflets, is called the *rhachis*, but if the frond is simple, that is, undivided, it is then called the rib or *costa*. These stipites, &c., are often more or less clothed with membranous scales, especially at their base, and as these often furnish means of recognising one kind from another, in gathering care should be taken not to rub them off.

When a frond is separated into distinct leaflets and these are simple it is said to be *pinnate*, should these leaflets or *pinnæ* as they are termed be again divided into leaflets the frond is said to be *bi-pinnate*, or twice leafletted, and so on *tripinnated*, &c., but when these divisions are connected at their base by their leafy blades the frond is termed *pinnatifid* and its division *lobes*, the terms *bi-pinnatifid tri-pinnatifid* being used in description ; fronds that are very much divided are usually termed *decompound*. The fronds are traversed by a series of veins, the midrib of the *frond* or *pinna* is called the *costa* or costule, the first series of branches from which are called *veins*, the secondary series the *venules*, and the third series, the *veinlets*. This arrangement is called the *venation* and has according to its various forms received distinguishing names, thus when the veins are unbranched they are said to be *simple*. Some= times they are branched once or more and are then said to be *forked* or *pinnately costaform*, that is, resembling a midrib, and having the *venules* or branches either forked or simple. When they are alike on both sides of the midrib they are said to be equal, if without a midrib they are called *radiate*, if produced from one side of a marginal midrib *excentric*. In all these cases the apices of the veins may terminate at or within the margin of the frond or its divisions, when they are said to be *direct* and free ; but similar forms of venation may occur, having the apices of the veins of either the first, second or third series combined in some way or other, thus if the whole system of venation is uniformly combined, so as to form a network, it is said to be *reticulated* ; if the simple or forked veins are united by a continuous vein parallel with or close to the margin it is said to be *transverse marginal*. Sometimes the apices of the venules of one series or fascicle combine with the apices of the adjoining series, this is called *anastomosing;* of this arrangement there are some modifications as *angular* and *arcuate* or arched anastomosing, which are further modified by producing from their exterior side other outwardly-directed *excurrent* veins or veinlets, which are either free, terminating in the *areoles* (meshes) or margin, or anastomose with the next superior venule. In some forms of netted venation, the venules are irregularly combined, the areoles or meshes producing from their sides certain simple or forked variously-directed veinlets, which terminate· within the unequal-sided meshes, this arrangement is called *compound anastomosing*. When the veins are somewhat elevated above the fronds surface they are said to be *external*, and when indistinct from their immersion in the fronds substance *internal*.

From some part of the venation the fructification is produced, where this occurs the part will become thickened, this part is called the *receptacle*, and if situated at the apex of the vein or venule is said to be *terminal*, between the base and apex *medial*, if seated on the angular crossing, or point of confluence of two or more venules or veinlets, *compital*.

It consists, in most cases of one-celled spore-cases, *sporangia*, or seed cases, more or less completely girt by an elastic ring, but in some cases of sporangia which are many-celled or destitute of the ring.

These spore-cases are mostly collected into masses which usually consist of multitudes of crowded spore-cases and is called a *sorus*, but being usually spoken of collectively the plural term *sori* will be more frequently met with ; these sori are either round or elongated, but sometimes they are of no determinable form when they are called *amorphous*. In most cases they are *dorsal* on the back of the frond, but sometimes they are marginal, or extra-marginal. The elongated sori are oblong, linear or continuous, and either form an angle with the midrib when they are said to be *oblique*, or run parallel with the margin or midrib. In some groups of ferns the sori are entirely exposed on the surface of the frond, while others have the sori covered more or less by a thin skin called *indusium* or *involucre* of which there are various modifications—as cupshaped, vaulted, &c., &c. The foregoing remarks on the structure of a fern will be found in accordance with the views of most writers on the subject, and will assist the student not only to better understand this work but any other on the same subject.

ON COLLECTING.

The feathery fern, the feathery fern,
An emerald sea it waveth wide,
And seems to flash, and gleam and burn,
Like the gentle flow of a golden tide ;
On a bushy slope or a leafy glade,
Amid the twilight depth of shade,
By interlacing branches made.
And trunks with lichens glorified.—*Anne Pratt*.

A FEW REMARKS ON COLLECTING AND CULTIVATING FERNS.

In collecting specimens for cultivation to insure success with kinds having underground running stems, such for instance as the tall scrub Maidenhair, it is necessary to select only close growing portions for removal, the way to find which is to follow the course of some creek until a place is found where a quantity of the surface soil has been washed away and the running stems of the plant desired either left bare or quite near the surface, here select portions of the rootstock for removal. With those of a tufted growth it is also better to select plants found growing on old rotten logs than such as are found growing in the ground, although these latter will likely appear much healthier. As each kind is collected carefully shake off the soil, wrap up each plant in soft wet paper and stow them away in the collecting bag ; this mode will be found far preferable to the usual way of carrying home a quantity of soil with each plant.

It is most necessary with ferns that they should be planted quite shallow. The growing point of rootstock should be kept well above the earth's surface. To accomplish this is not easy except the planter has some experience, the following will be found an effective way to remedy the evil of deep planting. Take two small pieces of rock or broken pot, place the fibrous roots of the fern with a sprinkle of fine soil between these, plant altogether holding the mass tight with the thumb and finger of the left hand while the outer soil is pressed close by the right. As a rule most terrestial species succeed best when planted out on rockwork the form of which must depend much upon the place it is to occupy and taste of person forming it, the primary thing to bear in mind is that the situation be well sheltered. The rock used in building should be of a hard porus nature, the spaces between the larger portions of rock should be well filled in with smaller portions of the same material mixed with good light scrub soil, to which if possible add a small quantity of broken charcoal and white sand. Be careful that the drainage is complete as no fern will thrive where water is allowed to stagnate about its roots.

In planting care should be taken to give to each kind a situation as near as possible resembling that in which it would be found occupying in its natural habitat, paying attention to this will impart to the whole a natural and graceful appearance.

When cultivated in pots the following rules should be observed: for drainage use plenty of broken pieces of brick, or lumps of sandstone mixed with charcoal, this might fill say one third of the pot, for compost use say equal parts of scrub soil, cut or beaten up old masses of bird's nest or staghorn ferns, and silver or white sand to which might be added with advantage a small quantity of small pieces of broken brick.

Those species which grow naturally against rocks or on trees and are called epiphytes, in transplanting, should be carefully and firmly fixed to some mass of rock, stone or wood to which, should the situation prove suitable, they will soon firmly adhere by fresh rootlets.

Several of our more hardy species might be planted in shady, sheltered, moist situations in the garden or shubbery where they would require no more attention than ordinary garden plants; after planting give a thorough watering and carefully shade.

THE

QUEENSLAND FERNS,

GROUPED ACCORDING TO THEIR NATURAL HABITAT.

> " The desire which tends to know
> The works of God thereby to glorify
> The Great Workmaster leads no excess,
> That reaches blame, but rather merits praise
> The more it seems excess,   ·
> For wonderful indeed are all His works,
> Pleasant to know, and worthiest to be all
> Had in remembrance always with delight."—*Milton.*

Group I. CLIMBING FERNS, and those also found climbing by means of adventitious rootlets.

II. CREEKSIDE FERNS, or those usually found by watercourses.

III. EPIPHYTAL FERNS, such as are found upon trees, and whose roots are independent of the ground.

IV. FOREST FERNS, those usually met with in timbered country.

V. ROCK FERNS, those found on damp or dry rocks.

VI. SCRUB FERNS, in this group will be found those which require a deep rich soil.

VII. SWAMP FERNS, kind either growing in water or very close to it.

VIII. TREE FERNS, arborescent kind such as form trunk-like stems of various height.

GROUP I.—CLIMBING FERNS.

Lygodium reticulatum. A tropical kind with glossy green leaves, the veins of which are netted. Found in dense scrubs climbing high up the trees.

Lygodium japonicum. This fern somewhat resembles the last but may easily be distinguished by its free veins. It is also usually found along the banks of watercourses in tropical Queensland.

Lygodium scandens. This beautiful species enjoys a much wider range, being met with around swamps from the Tweed River to Cape York, its leaves are much smaller than the former kinds, veins free like the last.

Acrostichum scandens. A strong woody rampant species found climbing the trees in our tropical swamps, leaves large pinnate.

CLIMBERS BY ADVENTITIOUS ROOTLETS.

Trichomanes peltatum. A Trinity Bay species, the round glittering skinlike leaves of this delicate kind adheres to the bark of the scrub trees like fish scales.

Trichomanes vitiense, on bark of scrub trees, tropical and extratropical, leaves skinlike, oblong or lobed small.

Aspidium ramosum. A beautiful pinnate leaved fern of wide range, found from the Illawarra to Endeavour River. The seed patches covered by a kidney shaped skin.

Polypodium tenellum. A south Queensland fern somewhat similar to the last from which it is at once known by the absence of covering to seed patches.

Polypodium scandens. A much more robust fern, leaves simple or deeply lobed. Found from the Gellibrand River in Victoria to the Maroochie in Queensland.

Grammitis ampla. This is the most imposing occupant of the stems of trees in our tropical scrubs. Leaves often more than three feet long, very broad and deeply lobed.

Acrostichum sorbifolium var. leptocarpum. Leaves very long pinnate of a deep green colour and numerous leaflets, of two forms fertile and sterile, often found with the last which it equals in elegance.

Group II.—Creekside Ferns.

Marattia fraxinea, and **Angiopteris evecta,** are two superb ferns found in close deep gullies usually near running water in the tropics. The immense succulent leaves and large globose scaly base of these ferns are one of the most imposing sights of tropical vegetation.

Trichomanes rigidum. This dark green bristle fern may be often met bordering the running water of mountain creeks in Queensland. It has also been gathered in N. S. Wales.

Dicksonia davallioides. This beautiful fern is of very delicate texture, although the fronds often attain two or three feet in height. They arise from an underground running stem, the fern is not very common in Queensland, but is to be met with along some of the sandy creeks, for instance, Enoggera. It is found more abundantly in N. S. Wales and has also been met with in Victoria.

Davallia dubia. This is a much more robust plant than the last having more harsh foliage, it differs also in having a short thick rootstock, and is of very common occurrence along sandy creeks and hillsides. It is also common to Tasmania, Victoria and N. S. Wales.

Adiantum æthiopicum. Common maiden-hair, very common along creeksides.

Lomaria Patersoni, often found on mountain creek banks, leaves narrow tapering and sometimes deeply lobed from a short rootstock.

Lomaria discolor. This beautiful fern has much the habit of a tree fern, stem one foot high, leaves a light green, deeply cut into rounded lobes almost to the polished black midrib; only Queensland habitat at present known Fern Creek, Maroochie and Rockingham Bay.

Blechnum cartilagineum. Found on grassy banked creeks throughout Queensland, also in N. S. Wales and Victoria, leaves one or two feet long deeply divided into close tapering lobes, the rootstock black and rough.

Blechnum orientale. The leaves of this very handsome fern are often five or six feet high pinnate and very graceful.. It is usually met with in close deep gullies near running water, tropical Queensland.

Aspidium molle. This lovely soft leaved pinnate fern is one of the most common which one meets with along watercourses in Queensland.

Polypodium irioides. This iris like leaved fern forms quite a margin to some of the rivers of Northern Queensland.

GROUP III.—EPIPHYTES, OR THOSE GROWING ON TREES.

Ophioglossum pendulum. This species, which is at once known by its ribbon-like leaves, is usually met with growing in the old masses of other ferns on scrub trees throughout the colony of Queensland.

Davallia pyxidata, or hare's-foot fern, is usually met with, like the last, growing out of the mass formed by some other fern or in the forks of scrub trees; the leaves are much divided, of a deep color, and of a hard gristle-like consistence. Found throughout Queensland and N. S. Wales.

Vittaria elongata. This is a grass-like fern found on the stems of scrub trees, most abundant in the tropics, where its leaves often reach the length of two or three feet long, and half-an-inch broad, but at Maroochie the leaves are much narrower and are seldom more than six inches long. This fern is also found on the trees of the Richmond and Macleay Rivers' scrubs, N. S. Wales.

Lindsæa lanuginosa. A very showy fern, forms one of the largest masses of all the Epiphytes found on Queensland trees. Its leaves are pinnate and often three or four feet long, and when young covered with a soft wool. Not met with out of the tropics, and seldom met with in cultivation.

Asplenium nidus.—Birds nest fern. Leaves often very long strap-like, the mid-rib usually dark and glossy. Very large plants of this fern may be met with oftentimes on rock in the close gullies of the Queensland ranges. The fern is also of frequent occurrence in N. S. Wales.

Asplenium simplicifrons. This fern resembles the young drawn up plants of the birds-nest fern, but may be distinguished by the absence of the vein near the edge of the leaf which in that fern joins the transverse veins together. Found on trees from Rockingham Bay to the Trinity Bay Ranges.

Asplenium falcatum. One of the most graceful of all the kinds found on Australian scrub trees; leaves pinnate, glossy, dark green, often six feet long, drooping; mostly found growing out of old masses of birds-nest fern. Common in scrubs from the Illawarra, N, S, Wales, to Rockingham Bay, Queensland.

Aspidium cordifolium. Commonly found growing in the masses of Epiphytes both in Queensland and N. S. Wales. This plant, which is equally common on rocks, is directly recognized by the bright glossy *tubors* which are formed on its wiry running stems.

Polypodium serpens. A small thick-leaved matted fern found growing on trees in swamps, most plentiful near the coast from Cape Howe, Victoria, to Rockingham Bay, Queensland.

Polypodiun confluens. In texture this plant resembles the last, but its leaves are often six to eight inches long. Common on scrub trees in Queensland and N. S. Wales. The seed patches of this and the last kind are large and often run together at the ends of the thick leaves in one mass.

Polypodium acrostichoides. The same thick leaves as the last but much longer, stiffer and often forked, the seed patches are also much smaller. Found on trees along the tropical coast of Queensland.

Polypodium attenuatum. Found on trees in the ranges of both Queensland and N. S. Wales. Leaves thick, dark green, narrow; the seed patches oval, large forming raised marks on the upper surface.

Polypodium simplicissimum. Leaves tapering, six inches long, on stems of trees, Rockingham Bay, Queensland.

Polypodium subauriculatum. A very beautiful pinnate leaved fern found on the trees of tropical Queensland, forming at times large patches. The leaves are of delicate texture and have a graceful weeping habit.

Platycerium alcicorne, or elk's horn. Plants of this kind are often clustered together in immense masses. The leaves (fronds) are of two forms, those bearing the seed patches being divided into long lobes, at the points of which the seed patches are placed.

Platycerium grande, or stag's horn, is a much larger plant and is more frequently found singly, the fertile leaves or those bearing the seed patches are from the crown and often very large, the seed patches of this kind will be found situated at the first large bay of these widely divided leaves. Both this and the last are common to the scrubs of Queensland and N. S. Wales.

GROUP IV.—FOREST FERNS.

Ophioglossum vulgatum. There are two forms of this common adder's tongue, met with in forest or timbered country usually on the damp flats or the western slope of a hill. In these situations the plant is seldom above four inches high and often not more than an inch, the fertile portion similiar in each but the sterile frond varies much in form being in some narrow and grass-like, an inch and a half long, while in others it will be found nearly round and not more than a quarter of an inch across. Roots hard brittle-tubers. Common throughout Queensland, N. S. Wales, Victoria and Tasmania.

o

Botrychium ternatum. This curious plant has the same form of hard brittle tuberous root as the last, but the barren portion of its leaf resembles somewhat a leaf of parsley. The fertile portion is erect and would convey to one the idea that it was the same form blighted. Whole plant from one to two feet high. Same range as last but usually met with on the small rich flats of ranges.

Schizæa bifida. A harsh grasslike fern, leaves simply forked growing in dense tufts on dry forest land from N. Australia through Queensland, N. S. Wales, Victoria and Tasmania. To the non-botanical collector the fertile portion at the tips of the divisions of leaves may be mistaken for a galled portion of the frond.

Davallia dubia, which has been noticed under creekside ferns will often be met with in forest country, especially on hill sides where the land is of a rich nature.

Lindsæa dimorpha. This pretty little tufted fern which so far as at present known is peculiar to Queensland, is usually met with on damp sandy soil under the shade of trees. The localities are Eight Mile Plains, Kedron Brook, Gympie road, and near the summit of one of the Glasshouse Mountains. The leaves are ot two forms, those at the base usually sterile and only two or three inches long, and several in a rather dense tuft. The fertile leaves are much taller, often eight or nine inches high, bearing half-moon like leaflets.

Lindsæa microphylla. This elegant fern often forms tufts of its delicate much divided leaves of from a foot to two feet high on the sides of hills and dry creek banks in the forest country of Southern Queensland and N. S. Wales.

Lindsæa incisa. It would be difficult to find a more delicately beautiful fern than this, the hair like running stems are so matted together that the feather-like leaves come up close together and form quite a carpet under the sheaoakes on sandy land its favourite habitat. Found in plenty on the Brisbane race-course. Peculiar to Queensland.

Adiantum hispidulum, or rough maiden hair. A tufted pretty fern found commonly by the side of logs in forest country throughout Queensland, N. S. Wales and Victoria.

Hypolepis tenuifolia. A tall growing fern often much branched forming thickets in the close gullies of the ranges both in Queensland and N. S. Wales. May often be mistaken for another fern Polypodium punctatum.

Cheilanthes tenuifolia and its variety **Sieberi** are two very brittle ferns met with in forest country, the latter has a much narrower leaf and in south Queensland is the commoner of the two. The species is more plentiful in northern Queensland where also another form is met with called **nudiuscula.** One or other form of this fern is found in all the Australian Colonies.

Pteris aquilina var esculenta. The common bracken is the most universal of ferns, but the Australian variety is said to belong exclusively to the southern hemisphere.

Pteris incisa, or bat's wing fern, is a tall light coloured fern often seen on the western side of hills in southern Queensland and throughout the other Australias, with Tasmania.

Doodia caudata. A most common fern in Queensland, is also plentiful in N. S. Wales, Vietoria and Tasmania, very various as to form as will be seen by referring to the botanical part of this work.

Polypodium punctatum. Very like Hypolepis and for which it may be mistaken, if the seed patches be not observed, is a tall soft hairy fern with running rootstock. Queensland, N. S. Wales, Victoria and Tasmania.

GROUP V.—ROCK FERNS.

Gleichenia dicarpa. Stem wiry trailing over damp rocks, leaves large intricately divided, covered with small round leaflets. Petrie's quarries near Brisbane to Rockingham Bay in Queensland, also in many parts of N. S. Wales, Vietoria and Tasmania.

Trichomanes parvulum. A beautiful moss-like bristle fern, found on many wet rocks in shady places in Queensland, as Enoggera, Maroochie and Trinity Bay range. The plant is also found on trees.

Trichomanes pyxidiferum Leaves transparent about two inches long from a closely matted running stem, found covering the rocks in the beds of creeks in the ranges of tropical Queensland.

Trichomanes parviflorum. Leaves very much divided into narrow lobes, whole leaf three to six inches high, found on the damp rocks of Rockingham Bay, Queensland.

Hymenophyllum javanicum. The frilled stalked film fern. Is found on damp rocks also at Rockingham Bay, in Queensland, Blue Mountains, N. S. Wales, and in several parts of Victoria and Tasmania.

Hymenophyllum tunbridgense or Tunbridge filmi fern. This well known and favourite British fern seems only to have been met with in one locality in Queensland, Mount Lindsey, but it is more plentiful in N. S. Wales, Victoria and Tasmania.

Davallia pedata. This lovely creeping fern clothes the rocks somewhat like ivy, where it is found, but it is not very plentiful. Mount Graham, Herbert River, Rockingham Bay, Queensland.

Lindsæa linearis. A brittle pinnate, narrow, erect leaved fern often found growing in the crevices of rocks at Stanthorpe and Moreton Bay in Queensland. Is more general in all the other Australian colonies and Tasmania.

Lindsæa cultrata L. flabellulata and L lobata, are pretty close growing ferns which are found on damp rocks in several parts of tropical Queensland. The first also grows on the rocks at Maroochie.

Adiantum lunulatum on rocks, Rockingham Bay. This Maidenhair fern is simply pinnate, leaflets large, somewhat crescent-shaped. The leaf frequently bearing a young plant at its end.

Adiantum capillus-veneris. The British Maiden-hair fern. This well known and wide spread fern has only been met with in one place in Australia, on the wet rocks near Northampton, according to Flora Australia, Vol. VII, page 723, which is probably a mistake; for our common species, A. hispidulum, when found on rocks in dense shade, is, while young, very similar to it, the leaflets being on such plants often deeply cut.

Adiantum affine. A strong growing handsome Maiden-hair fern, found creeping over the rocks in bed of the Maroochie River, and creeks in Queensland, and also in several places in N. S. Wales.

Pteris falcata. A beautiful brittle stalked fern often found among dry loose rocks in the ranges, leaves from a foot to a foot and a half long, with many hard dark green leaflets. The form and also size of the pinnæ varies considerably in this species; a smaller form of more tufted growth, is one of the commonest ferns met with on damp rocks; this small form is figured in "Species Filicum" plate III, as Pellæa falcata var. nana. One or other form of the species is met with in Queensland, N. S. Wales, Victoria and Tasmania.

Pteris longifolia. A fine tall erect leaved tufted fern. Leaves of many long narrow tapering leaflets. Found on the rocks of the Main Range, Cunningham's Gap and Rockhampton in Queensland, Blue Mountains and other parts of N. S. Wales, and also in Victoria.

Monogramme junghuhnii, on damp rocks, Rockingham Bay. This curious narrow leaved fern might be mistaken for a tuft of grass. Queensland.

Doodia caudata. A most variable fern, very common to both dry and wet rocks; leaves at times stiff and erect, but commonly very thin, weak, and lying on the surface of rock; the end of leaf lengthened out and somewhat tail-like, whence the name. Very abundant in Queensland, N. S. Wales, Victoria and Tasmania.

Asplenium nidus, the Bird's nest fern, is quite as often seen on rocks as on trees, in which group it has been already noticed. The same may be said of **A. simplicifrons,** already noticed.

Asplenium attenuatum, may be found on old damp rocks in shady places in Southern Queensland and N. S. Wales. The plant is of a tufty habit, the leaves long and tapering to the point where it often produces a young plant; they are entire or very much cut up into lobes on which account one variety is named multi lobum, another variety found at Maroochie is always entire, after which feature it is named.

Asplenium flabellifolium. A pretty little tufted fern found on damp rocks, Enoggera Creek, and also Dalrymple Creek, Queensland, and in many parts of N. S. Wales, South Australia, Victoria, Western Australia and Tasmania. Its delicate hair-like leaf stalk and fan shaped leaflets make it a general favourite in cultivation. It suits admirably for hanging baskets.

Asplenium paleaceum, is very like the much divided form of

A. attenuatum. but is much more hairy and covered usually with scales. On wet rocks in many parts of tropical Queensland.

Asplenium laserpitiifolium. The most graceful of all the Australian Aspleniums. The leaves are much divided, the stalks polished, black, habit of plant tufted, with tall leaves the upper portion of which falls outwards in a beautiful curve. On rocks, &c., Northern Queensland scrubs.

Aspidium cordifolium The well known bulbous fern of Queensland rocks, also found growing in the mass formed on trees by other plants. Also in several places in New South Wales. A useful fern for growing in hanging baskets, being very hardy.

Aspidium exaltatum. A very large fern found rambling over the rocks of the tropical Queensland coast, leaves often six feet high. This fern in growth resembling the garden strawberry by sending out weak runners at the end of which a plant is formed so soon as it is caught in the crevice of rock.

Polypodium australe. A very small densely matted fern growing on damp rocks, Maroochie, Queensland, and many parts of N. S. Wales, Victoria and Tasmania.

Polypodium Hookeri. Rather larger than the last, but like that species forming a dense mat on the damp rocks, Rockingham Bay Ranges, Trinity Bay in Queensland; also Lord Howe's Island, N. S. Wales.

Polypodium subauriculatum. Stem thick, shortly creeping over rocks; leaves thin pinnate two or three feet long, somewhat weeping in habit; this handsome fern is also found growing on trees in many parts of tropical Queensland. Is a handsome fern and easy to cultivate either on rockwork or in hanging baskets.

Polypodium rigidulum. Is the most universal rock fern in Queensland, and is well known by the great difference in appearance between its two forms of leaves. The short broad dry form is often gathered for decorative purposes. This is another fern which is admirably adapted for growing in hanging baskets, the great diversity of its foliage making it always an object of interest, and another great advantage is it will bear a much more exposed situation than most other ferns. Found on dry rock throughout Queensland, and Blue Mountains, N. S. Wales.

Notholæna distans. A small hairy fern found on exposed rocks in many parts of Queensland, N. S. Wales, Victoria, South Australia, and Western Australia.

Notholæna vellea is a larger plant, more hairy or woolly, which is met with on rocks throughout tropical Australia, and in a few extratropical places. The plant is difficult to cultivate but very handsome.

Grammitis Muelleri. A most beautiful fern with a very variable foliage, which is densely covered on the back with scaly hairs; the plant is peculiar to Queensland and may be found in abundance on the rocks of the hills about Cleveland Bay, and many other parts of tropical Queensland. This very desirable plant has lately been most successfully cultivated by Mr. Pink, gardener to the Queensland Acclimatisation Society.

Grammitis rutæfolium. A small tufted fern met with on damp rocks throughout Australia and Tasmania.

Antrophyum reticulatum. This fern is found on damp rocks in many parts of tropical Queensland. In appearance it resembles the plantain or rib-grass.

Acrostichum conforme, or Deer's tongue fern is another simple leaved fern found on rocks about Rockingham Bay, &c.

Both the species of Platycerium are found on rocks, but are seen to greater perfection on trees under which heading they have been noticed.

GROUP VI.—SCRUB FERNS.

Gleichenia dichotoma. A large handsome rambling fern found on the borders of scrubs, where the soil is swampy, from Port Jackson around the coast to Port Darwin.

Davallia speluncæ. A large fern of somewhat rambling habit, leaves much divided and flaccid, found in tropical Queensland on the borders of scrubs.

Adiantum formosum. The tall Maiden-hair fern, very abundant in Queensland and N. S. Wales and a few places in Victoria. Leaves much divided, stalks shiny black.

Pteris paradoxa. This curious fern has a running underground stem from which arises leaves varying much in shape and size, at times only a few inches high, and bearing a single leaflet, at other times bearing from five to nine rather large oval leaflets which when fertile have a broad band of seed-patch around their edge which adds greatly to their beauty. Common to the scrubs of Queensland and N. S. Wales.

Pteris umbrosa. A handsome fern of mountain scrubs, plant tufted rootstock thick leaves tall dark green deeply lobed. Southern Queensland and N. S. Wales, and also Genoa River, Victoria.

Pteris tremula. A fine fern, leaves tall erect, much divided stalks polished, brown, very abundant in the scrubs of Queensland, N. S. Wales, Victoria and Tasmania.

Pteris quadriaurita. Of tufted growth like the last, leaves of much fewer divisions. Found in the scrubs of tropical Queensland.

Pteris marginata. Rootstock thick raising slightly from the ground, leaves very large divided into three divisions which are again divided into numerous lobes; one of the most imposing ferns of the scrubs of North Queensland.

Pteris comans. Is a somewhat similar fern to the last, but the leaves are much more branched and are not of so succulent a nature as that kind. The present kind is found in Southern Queensland and N. S. Wales, Victoria and Tasmania.

Asplenium umbrosum, or Caraway-seed fern. A large spreading plant from a stout short rootstock. Leaves broad generally of a succulent nature on the back of which the seed patches are in the form of caraway-seeds covered over with a thin skin.

Asplenium australe. Is a similar plant but may be distinguished by its more delicate leaves, smaller rootstock, and by the stalks being generally darker colored. Both are met with in the dense scrubs of Queensland, N. S. Wales, Victoria and Tasmania.

Asplenium decussatum. Stem short erect leaves broad often bearing bulbs (gemmæ) on the midrib. Rockingham Bay, Daintree River, &c., Queensland.

Aspidium pteroides. A tall handsome leaved fern with running underground stem, leaves with many long spreading leaflets. Seed patches near the edge covered by a thin kidney-shaped skin. Found in scrubs Rockingham Bay, and at foot of range Smithfield Barron River, Trinity Bay, Queensland.

Aspidium confluens. Stem short erect crowned by many broad leaves deeply lobed, on long dark colored stalks. This is one of the most showy ferns of our north Queensland scrubs, plentiful at Rockingham Bay and Trinity Bay Ranges, Johnstone and Daintree Rivers.

Aspidium aculeatum. A coarse leaved, often densely scally, fern. Found at head of Dalrymple Creek, South Queensland and in many parts of N. S. Wales, Victoria and Tasmania.

Aspidium aristatum. Stem creeping, leaves glossy, stalks hairy at the base, edge of leaf bordered by teeth ending in bristle-like points. Found in a few places in Queensland and N. S. Wales.

Aspidium decompositum. A most variable fern, both hairy and not hairy. The scale covering the seed-patches at times large and prominent, but on some plants quite small. The whole plant usually of a dark color. Found in most of the Queensland scrubs, in N. S. Wales, Victoria, Tasmania and also South Australia.

Aspidium tenerum. A very handsome and distinct kind, but at times may be mistaken for the last, the leaves being similarly divided into many parts, but the seed-patches will be observed to be placed very near to the margin. Found in scrubs from Moreton to Keppel Bays in Queensland, and in several of the northern scrubs of N. S Wales.

Aspidium tenericaule, Thw. Rootstock stout thick, very shortly creeping, covered with soft scale s. Leaves tall of delicate texture, stalks thick light colored also very scally while young. This fine fern should rather be placed under the genus Polypodium. Found in Three-mile scrub near Brisbane, in some of the tropical scrubs of Queensland, and also the Clarence River, N. S. Wales.

Polypodium urophyllum. Stem running underground sending up at distant intervals tall pinnate leaves, bearing leaflets, at times nearly a foot in length, having very regular veins joined to each other by their ends, seed-patches round in regular rows. Found in mountain scrubs of tropical Queensland.

Polypodium Hillii. A very handsome and rare fern, leaves large tall densely covered with short soft hairs. Found near Cleveland Bay, Queensland.

Polypodium pœcilophlebium. At times this fern might be mistaken for P. urophyllum, with which it is often found, but the direction of its veins are always very irregular and it is of much smaller habitat. Scrubs of tropical Queensland.

Polypodium nigrescens. Stem creeping thick, leaves tall broad and deeply lobed, the seed-patches deeply sunk in the leaf and forming raised lumps on the upper surface. Daintree River, Queensland.

Polypodium phymatodes. A fern very similar to the last, leaf perhaps of a thicker substance and vein not so prominent. Often found near the coast of tropical Queensland.

Polypodium verrucosum. Leaves tall pinnate, smooth leaflets long narrow, mark of seed-patches prominent on the upper surface of leaflet. Rockingham Bay, Daintree River.

Acrostichum repandum. Stem creeping, leaves tall, leaflets four or five inches long often lobed, leaflets of fertile leaves much smaller. Several of the scrubs of tropical Queensland.

A. neglectum. Is certainly one of the most beautiful of our ferns, I found it on a small flat in one of the gullies leading into the Barron River, Trinity Bay range. Its fronds are from two to three or even more feet high deeply cut into narrow lobes, which are furnished on the margin with teeth like a saw, the stalks are frilled to the base, and the whole frond of a rich deep green color.

Group VII.—Swamp Ferns.

Helminthostachys zeylanica. Rookstock shortly creeping. The leaf from six to eighteen inches high, tender spread out somewhat like a hand on the top of the stalk, at the base of which arises a spike bearing the seed. This curious plant is most abundant around swamps from Rockhampton to the Barron River, Trinity Bay, Queensland.

Schizæa Forsteri· A small and beautiful fern often found growing among the roots of tall palms in swamps. Leaf fan shaped from three to six inches high, divided into narrow lobes crowned by star shaped brown seed patches, rest of plant a bright green. Found at the base of palms at Maroochie, and also Trinity Bay ranges.

Ceratopteris thalictroides. A water fern found growing in the still waters of swamps and also on the damp soil around. Leaves from a short thick crown much and irregularly divided into narrow stalk-like lobes; the whole of a very pale color. Found from Brisbane River to Port Darwin, most abundant around the Barron River.

Gleichenia circinata. A tall intricately branched fern found around swamps on sandy lands ; the underneath part of leaf of a pale color. Found in all the colonies except Western Australia.

Pteris geraniifolia. A very pretty tufted fern. Leaves resembling those of the lobed leaved geranium or vine, two to six inches high, stalks dark, as are also the main veins of the leaf. This plant is often found growing on the hillocks formed by grass or other plants in swamps ; from the Brisbane River to Rockingham Bay. It is most abundant on some of the damp hills off the Pioneer River, and is also met with in New England and N. S. Wales.

Lomaria capensis. A strong coarse fern, often forming a trunk of several feet in height. Leaves long erect of two forms, pinnate leaflets of barren leaves, rough. Found from Eight-mile Plains, near Brisbane, to Rockingham Bay in Queensland ; common in swampy parts of N. S. Wales, Victoria, South Australia, (Mt. Lofty ranges) and also Tasmania.

Blechnum serrulatum. Rootstock long creeping, often running up under the loose bark of tea-tree ; leaves long on long stalks, pale colored, the upper part bearing harsh linear leaflets the edge of which finely toothed, seed patches near the mid-rib. Found through Queensland round to Port Darwin and also in N. S. Wales.

Asplenium sylvaticum. A short erect scaly rootstock, leaves one or two feet long, pinnate. Damp places, Rockingham Bay.

Asplenium maximum and **Asplenium polypodioides** are two strong growing ferns which at times form a trunk of several feet in height crowned at the summit, and some distance down their trunks with large spreading leaves six or more feet long, and two or more feet wide. Both are met with in the swamps of Northern Queensland and the first in several parts of N. S. Wales.

Aspidium unitum. Stem creeping beneath the surface ; leaves erect, the upper portion only with leaflets which are from two to six inches long ; one form of this plant is quite downy at times but scarcely persistently enough to form a good variety. The plant is common to all the swamps of Queensland, is found also in many parts of N. S. Wales, and also Western Australia.

Acrostichum aureum. A tall fern of a yellowish hue, rootstock short thick ; leaves pinnate, often six feet high, many together, forming large clumps in salt marshes ; on young plants the leaves are very frequently simple, that is formed of a single leaflet. Found from Port Darwin along the coast and up the river so far as the tide reaches through Queensland to the rivers Clarence and Richmond in N. S. Wales. A remarkable feature with this fine plant is that it will succeed under cultivation without the aid of saline influence.

GROUP VIII.—TREE FERNS.

Todea barbara. This might have been placed equally well with swamp kinds but at times it may be seen with a trunk of even more than six feet in height and two feet in diameter, thus proving its right to rank with tree ferns. The leaves with which this stout trunk is crowned are twice pinnate, and often more than six feet long ; the seed patches are placed on the lower lobes of the second leaflets. Found in wet parts in many parts of Queensland, as

D

Eight-mile Plains, Moreton Bay, Maroochie, Rockingham Bay and also in several parts of N. S. Wales, Victoria aud Tasmania.

Cyathea Lindseyana. A tree fern of Mount Lindsey, said to have a trunk twelve feet high, four inches in diameter.

Cyathea arachnoidea. A tree fern of Rockingham Bay, said to form a trunk nearly twenty-one feet high. Few specimens seem to have been gathered of these two ferns and they are not known in cultivation.

Alsophila Rebeccæ. This is a very handsome tree with a rather slender trunk of about ten feet in height, often forming a mass of short stems at its base; leaves long and broad, of a rich dark green color. Found in close gullies, Rockingham Bay, Port Denison, Daintree River of tropical Queensland. Small plants of this kind under cultivation often produce fertile leaves which are also at times simply pinnate.

Alsophila australis. Trunk twenty feet high, stout leaves large spreading covered with scales while young. The commonest tree fern of Queensland, found both south and north; abundant also in N. S. Wales, Victoria and Tasmania. This fern is rather variable and on that account has been by some separated into several species.

Alsophila Leichhardtana. A tall rather slender stem tree fern, very dark and rough, leaves large and spreading, the stalks very rough. Abundant at Maroochie, Queensland, and several places in N. S. Wales.

Alsophila Robertsiana. A very distinct tree fern of Rockingham Bay, and Bellenden Ker Ranges. Stem about eight or ten feet high, leaves large and hairy.

Dicksonia antarctica. A tall tree fern, said to be at times fifty feet in height, stem very thick; leaves large broad harsh. Found in southern Queensland, N. S. Wales, Victoria, South Australia and Tasmania.

Dicksonia Youngiæ. A handsome tree fern, height about ten feet, leaves large glossy, the stalks at the bottom thickly covered with long brown hairs. Bellenden Ker in Queensland, several places of N. S. Wales. Some fragmentary specimens received from the Bunya Mountains appear to belong to this species.

Asplenium polypodioides often forms a trunk six or more feet high in the swamps of tropical Queensland, and might thus with propriety be placed among tree ferns as well as where it will be found with swamp kinds.

AUSTRALIAN FERNS

SYSTEMATICALLY ARRANGED.

" IF we give our children nothing but an amusing employment, we lose
the best half of our design ; which is, at the same time that we amuse
them, to exercise their understanding, and to accustom them to
attention. Before we teach them to name what they see, let us begin
by teaching them how to see. Suffer them not to think they know
anything of what is merely laid up in their memory." *Rousseau's
Letters on Botany.*

FOLLOWING the arrangement of the Filices or Ferns in the Flora
Australiensis we find them divided into six (6) tribes, the last of
which is again divided into two (2) sections, the one with, the other
without indusium, or covering to the sori, or seed-patches.

TRIBE I.—OPHIOGLOSSEÆ. This is the only tribe whose frond in
a young state are not rolled inwards (circinate). The barren frond
or portion of frond leaf-like, the fertile portion spike-like, simple or
branched, the stalks most frequently combined at the base. Spore-
cases globular, two-celled, without any ring, sessile (stalkless) in two
rows or in small clusters on the spike or its branches, Genera 3.

I.—OPHIOGLOSSUM LINN. OR ADDERS-TONGUE.

Fronds two-branched, the barren portion spreading leaf-like
entire or forked at the end, reticulated veins forming elongated
areoles, fertile portion spike-like simple stalked. Spore-cases sessile
(stalkless) and more or less combined back to back in two rows
along the rib, opening in a fissure transverse as to the spike,
longitudinal as to the spore-case. The name literally means the
same as the English, and is derived from the supposed resemblance
of the fertile spike to a serpent's tongue. There are two species of
this in Australia.

O. vulgatum, Linn. Common Adders-tongue. There are several
forms all having the same short fleshy rootstock which might be
compared to a miniature Dahlia root, but varying much in the size
and form of the frond. The combined frond usually solitary, but
occasionally sending up several fronds from the same rootstock,
from one to nine inches high, the barren leaf-like portion stalkless
(sessile) at or below the middle of the stipes (stalk), varying from
broadly ovate or oblong-lanceolate and a few inches long, to
roundish and not over a $\frac{1}{4}$ or $\frac{1}{2}$ inch, or very narrow-lanceolate or
linear, and one inch or more long. The veins when broad
copiously netted but in the narrow forms more longitudinal and but
slightly anastomosing, the fertile portion or tongue varying in size
with the plant as is the case with the spore-cases, sometimes there

being a very few, sometimes over a dozen in each row. The normal form, or the one with large broad blades, will be mostly met with in close damp gullies or beds of rivers, between ranges, often growing in the crevices of rocks. The other two forms are usually found growing among grass in damp localities all over Queensland, also in N. S. Wales, Victoria, Tasmania and N. Australia.

O. pendulum, Linn. Ribbon Fern. This plant is mostly found epiphytal on stag's-horn fern, its fronds long and fleshy often hanging like fleshy ribbons from the base of the plant upon which it is growing to the length of several feet, the ends are at times forked; about the middle of this long ribbon is situated the tongue-like fertile spike which is often short but at times six inches long and ¼ inch broad bearing two opposite rows of spore-cases as in the terrestrial species. The short fleshy roots of this species are very brittle, thus it is difficult to transplant without removing a large portion of the stag's-horn along with it, indeed it always seems to thrive best when growing in company with that fern. Found throughout Queensland and part of N. S. Wales.

II.—BOTRYCHIUM, SWARTZ. OR MOONWORT.

Fructification on a distinct branch of the frond paniculate with many one-sided spikelets spore-cases in two rows, globose separate, bursting transverse to the rib or branch on which they are placed longitudinal as to the spore-case.

Name derived from the Greek on account of the supposed resemblance of the fertile portion of the frond to a bunch of grapes. Two species are met with in Australia.

B. lunaria, Swartz. The common moonwort of Britain has not as yet been found in Queensland but is plentiful in Victoria and Tasmania. Size of plant varying from three to eight inches high, a few scales at the base, otherwise smooth erect, barren portion of frond pinnate one to three inches long, bearing from five to fifteen somewhat fan-shaped leaflets entire or notched at the margin, veins forked radiating from the base, fertile branch erect shortly branched; usually found on grassy plains.

B. ternatum, Swartz. Grape Fern. Roots often deep in the earth. Fertile and barren portions of frond often divided just above the crown of the plant; from six to eighteen inches high, fertile portions erect, barren portions spreading and much divided resembling a leaf of parsley, veins diverging but mostly hidden in the thick substance of the frond. Besides many parts of Queensland this fern is also met with in New South Wales, Victoria and Tasmania. The plant delights in a rich dark moist soil, and is therefore often met with along the banks of rivers; at one time it was abundant along the Brisbane. In the gullies of Taylor's range fine specimens may often be gathered.

III.—HELMINTHOSTACHYS, KAULF.

Fertile portion of frond consisting of an erect spike bearing small clusters of spore-cases around its stalk. Name derived from two Greek words on account of the fertile portion of frond being supposed to resemble a worm.

H. zeylanica, Hook. A fern common to the swamps of Northern Queensland, rootstock or rhizome thick horizontal one to six inches long, sending out thick hard fibres from the under surface; frond one to two feet high of two parts, the erect fertile portion stalked spike-like, often wanting; barren portion broad stalkless spreading divided mostly into three parts which are often again divided into long segments three to six inches long, half-inch to one-inch broad, these segments are at times slightly toothed (denticulated); veins simple or forked, diverging from the mid-rib. This plant in the Moluccas is regarded as a slight aperient, is used as a pot herb, the young shoots resembling asparagus.

TRIBE II.—MARATTIEÆ. The young growth rolled inwards (circinate) thus differing from Tribe I, but, like that tribe, having no jointed ring to the spore or seed cases; opening in two valves or in a longitudinal slit, sessile or united, in two rows; in the sori forming marginal lobes to the segments, or placed on their under surface.

IV.—LYGODIUM, SWARTZ. SNAKE'S TONGUE.

Beautiful climbing ferns, often met with along the edge of rivers and swamps, covering the shrubs and climbing to a great height up the surrounding trees by their twining stems or rather branched fronds, which bear pinnate (in the Australian species) branches in divaricate pairs. Pinnules of the barren portion from ovate to lanceolate; spore cases globular or transversely oblong, with longitudinal striæ at the upper end, opening in a longitudinal slip, sessile in two rows. Sori forming spike-like lobes on the border of pinnule, spore cases solitary within a scale. Name from Lygodes, flexible.

L scandens, Swartz. Climbing Snake fern. Rhizome cæspitose branches of frond conjugate, pinnate, pinnules few or many, varying in form from nearly heart shaped (cordate) to almost hastate, sometimes slightly lobed at the base; articulated on a short petiolule at the base of the lamina the petiolule remaining persistent on the rhachis after the pinnule has fallen. Veins free, forked free radicating, the central more or less costæ form. Sori in spikes around the edge of pinnules which are in other respects similar to the barren ones, spore-cases various in number on the same specimen. Common in or around swamps within a few miles of the coast, from the Tweed River to Port Darwin.

Lygodium reticulatum Schkuhr. Scrub Snake fern. Habit of plant similar to last but habitat very different, this species being usually found in the dense scrubs of tropical Australia climbing high up the tall trees like L. scandens, the pinnules are articulated upon the petiolule but they are usually much larger, more rigid,

and of a darker color. The veins are forked from a central costa,
venules anastomosing in unequal oblique-elongated, hexagonal
areoles. Sori in spike along edge of pinnule. Found on York
Peninsula, Daintree River, Rockingham Bay, Trinity Bay
Range, &c.

Lygodium japonicum, Swartz. Habit of plant similar to L.
scandens having the same form of climbing rhachis and conjugate
branches on short primary petioles, but the pinnules are much longer
and not articulated, the lower ones often pinnate, veins free. Sori
forming short linear marginal lobes as in the other species. This
species is very plentiful along the banks of rivers in tropical
Australia, and perhaps is found further inland than the other
species of the genus ; to those pteridologists who look to the
venation as a primary characteristic in classification, it will seem
out of place to find a fern with anastomosing veins placed between
two free veined species. But in the Flora Australiensis greater
importance seems to be attached to the articulation of the petiolule
than venation of the pinnule.

V.—SCHIZÆA, SM.

Rhizome cæspitose. Fronds erect, linear, terete, simple or
dichotomously forked. Sori forming small linear pinnules, closely
imbricate in a second spike at the end of the fertile segments,
those of the two sides folded against each other with the fructification inside. Spore-cases globular or bluntly ovate having a many-
rayed apical ring, opening in two valves, sessile in two rows
covering the inner surface of the pinnule which is really their under
side, though from the curvature of the spike it appears to be the
upper side. Name from schizo, to divide ; from its split fronds.

S. fistulosa, Labill. Fronds densely tufted, four to eight inches
high terete, undivided rough, spikes of the fertile ones about half
inch long, with six to twenty pair of oblong soriferous pinnules
scarcely more than a line long denticulate or shortly fringed, spore-
cases usually four to eight pair in each sorus. Found in heathy
places in Gipps-land and other parts of Victoria, also in many
places in Tasmania.

S. bifida, Swartz. Fronds densely tufted, terete six to eighteen
high, once forked at or about the middle or undivided, stipes often
chestnut brown. Spike of the fertile ones half to three-quarter
inches long the soriferous pinnules numerous and closely packed,
narrow-linear, three to four lines long fringed with cilia, spore-cases
often twenty pair much smaller than in S. fistulosa. Found in
North Australia, very common throughout Queensland on dry
forest land, plentiful in all parts of N. S. Wales, it is also met
with in Victoria and Tasmania.

S. rupestris, R. Br. Fronds about four inches high, undivided,
flattened about a line broad tapering to a short filiform stipes.
Fertile spike under half inch long, the soriferous pinnules six to

eight pair denticulate but not ciliate, the lower ones about two lines long and from that tapering to about one line. Spore-cases ten to twelve pair. Found on damp rocks in the Blue Mountains, Illawarra and Port Jackson, N. S. Wales.

S. dichotoma, Swartz. Rhizome shortly creeping, fronds six to eighteen inches high, firm erect, channelled above divided dichotomously, flabelliform in general outline four to nine inches broad, the segments of barren frond somewhat flattened segments of fertile frond narrower and each ending in a crest of soriferous pinnules as in S. bifida but the whole smaller. This curious sedge-like fern is found on the sandy land near the coast throughout Queensland to Port Darwin ; at times it may be met with growing in the crevices of rocks further inland and might then be mistaken for Psilotum triquetrum Sw ; specimens have also been gathered on the Blue Mountains and Parramatta, N. S. Wales.

S. Forsteri, Spreng. F. v. Muell Fragm VIII 275. Rhizome short scaly. Fronds three to nine inches high, glossy, Stipes light-colored channelled, the upper portion of frond dichotomously divided into four segments, which are rather broad for the size of the frond, glossy and taper to a neck like contraction at the apex thus giving a stipitate appearance to the fructification which is composed of from four to six hairy pinnules shorter than in S. dichotoma and placed digitato-pinnate not pectinato-pinnate as in that species, spore-cases biserial as in the other Australian species. The habitat of this species differs widely from that of the others it having only as yet been found in two places in Queensland, viz., Maroochie and Trinity Bay range, and in each of these places found growing amongst the roots of Palm trees which are often some distance above the level of the ground.

VI.—ANGIOPTERIS, HOFFMANN.

Rhizome, fleshy, subglobose, erect. Frond large, bi-pinnate, the stipes thick with two large auricles at the base. Spore-cases globular at first, laterally connected, afterwards free, without any ring, opening inwards in two valves, sessile in two close opposite rows forming an oblong sorus, these sori are placed side by side in a continuous row near the margin of the pinnules. No indusium.

A. evecta, Hoffm. Rhizome, a subglobose mass of a few feet high and thick, emitting thick fleshy cord-like roots from its base. Fronds bi-pinnate, very broad, twelve or more feet long, stipes thick pubescent, swollen and articulated at the base above the two leathery auricles which remain attached to the rhizome, pinnæ the lowest the largest, also swollen at the base of rhachis pinnules four to eight inches long, half-inch to one and half broad, abruptly acuminate, crenate serrate or at times entire, sessile or shortly stalked. Veins nearly parallel, diverging from the mid-rib entire or forked. Spore-cases four to six rows in each sorus. Found in close gullies Rockingham Bay, Daintree River, Trinity Bay ranges, Fitzroy Island, &c. One of the most noble of tropical ferns.

VII.—MARATTIA, SM.

Rhizome large globose, formed of the thick squamæ-form bases of fronds. Fronds large bi-tri-pinnate, the stipes with adnate auricules at base. Spore-cases completly united in two rows, in oblong boat-shaped sori placed side by side in a continuous row close to the edge of the pinnules or between the mid-rib and margin, the spore-cases opening inwards in longitudinal slits without any other external mark to distinguish them, the sorus appearing divided into so many cells in two rows. Name in honor of J. F. Maratti, of Tuscany, a writer upon Ferns.

M. fraxinea, Sm. Potatoe Fern. Pinnules oblong, lanceolate, acuminate, four to six inches long, half-inch to one and half broad, veins numerous, parallel simple or forked, points of barren pinnules often sharply serrated. Boat-shaped sori rather above a line long, oblique and close together in a continuous row close to the margin, the vein on which they rest sometimes slightly expanded and fringed but scarcely so in the Australian form ; upper surface of the sorus concave, the slits and cells indicating the number of united spore cases five to eight pairs in each sorus. In tropical Queensland this fern is often very abundant on the wet banks of mountain creeks seeming to delight in rich soil and dense scrub, also found on Lord Howe's Island, N. S. Wales, but this form is said to have smaller pinnules and longer sori of fifteen to twenty pair of spore-cases.

TRIBE III.—OSMUNDÆ. Fronds circinate in vernation, divided or compound. Spore-cases globular or nearly so, without any or with an imperfect or transverse ring, opening in two valves or irregularly, few, sometimes solitary, rarely many and clustered, in sori on the under surface of the segments or pinnules.

VIII.—CERATOPTERIS, BRONGN. WATER FERN.

Fertile fronds compound with narrow linear segments often proliferous. Sori of single globose spore-cases opening irregularly with an incomplete or rudimentary ring, inserted on longitudinal veins between the midrib and the margin of the segment in a loose manner. Indusium continuous and membranous, formed of the revolute margin of the segment. Spores large marked with concentric rings. Name from horn-like form of divisions of frond.

C. thalictroides, Brongn. (Meadow-rue leaved Water Fern). An annual aquatic or subaquatic tufted fern, fronds bi-tri-pinnate the fertile ones six to eighteen inches high, the secondary or tertiary pinnæ short, with few distinct linear segments three-quarter to above one inch long, the revolute margins enclosing the fructification the whole length. Barren fronds distinct, shorter and more spreading, with fewer short broad variously shaped segments, flat and of a soft half succulent texture usually of a light color. Spore-cases in the Australian form with a broad nearly complete ring. Plentiful in and around many of the swamps of tropical Queensland, both in water and on the damp land ; a few years ago plentiful near Brisbane, also found in North Australia.

IX.—PLATYZOMA, R. BR.

Rhizome horizontal, upon which the fronds are densely tufted, fronds pinnate, pinnæ small numerous. Sori of two to four spore-cases terminating simple veinlets proceeding from the midrib, the soriferous end free and incurved between the frond and an inner membrane. Spore-cases globular, very deciduous, bursting irregularly, the inner membrane of the pinna irregularly torn and disappearing. Name from the broad band of spore-case.

P. microphyllum, R. Br. Braid fern. Rhizome densely covered with long brown setaceous scales, fronds narrow, linear, rigid, six to twenty-four inches high. The rhachis smooth and glossy. Pinnæ exceedingly numerous, about a line long and broad ; the revolute margins almost closed over the midrib so as to give them a globular, or ovoid, bullate form, glabrous outside, powdery inside, especially on the midrib. Soriferous veins two or three on each side of the midrib. Found in several parts of North Australia and tropical Queensland, where on sandy hillocks it is said often to form a dense sward with its close, rigidly erect, fronds.

X.—GLEICHENIA, SM.

Fronds from a creeping rhizome erect or scrambling, the main rhachis dichotomous, with numerous entire or pinnatifid pinnules distichous along the ultimate branches and often also below the last forks. Sori without indusium of few (two to twelve) spore-cases attached to one branch of forked veinlets, either superficial or slightly embedded in the substance of the frond. Spore-cases surrounded by a transverse ring and opening vertically in 2 valves. Name in honor of K. W. F. von Gleichen, a German author on microscopic plants.

G. circinata, Swartz. Parasol Fern. Fronds sometimes short, but often repeatedly dichotomous and scrambling to the height of many feet, the main rhachis glabrous or shortly scaly-hirsute. Pinnules numerous along the ultimate branches, one to two inches long, pinnately divided into numerous ovate or almost orbicular segments, one to two lines diameter adnate by the broad base, often whitish underneath, flat on the margin more or less recurved or revolute. Sori of two to four, spore-cases superficial or half immersed in a slight cavity near the upper base or angle of the segments. This is the most widely spread of all the Australian species, being found in all the colonies. The form G. microphylla R. Br. has a more hairy rhachis and is wanting in the whitish covering to the under side of the segments. This form belongs to the southern colonies.

G. dicarpa, R. Br. Fronds like the small form of the last, with the rhachis glabrous or scaly-hispid, but the segments smaller almost globular and bullate, the revolute margins almost closed over to the rhachis, thus becoming saccata (pouch-like), sori of two

K

or rarely three spore-cases nearly concealed within the almost slipper-shaped segment in a broad cavity close to the rhachis and occupying more than half the breadth of the segment. Found in several parts of Queensland running over wet rocks, also in N. S. Wales, Victoria and Tasmania.

G. flabellata, R. Br. Fan Fern. Fronds tall, often six or more feet high, repeatedly dichotomous in fan-shaped branches. Pinnules numerous along the last branches and continued along the rhachis below the last fork, linear-lanceolate entire or the margins obscurely undulate, rarely much above one inch long, dilated and sometimes confluent at the base, one to one and a half lines broad, glabrous or with a few scaly hairs underneath, the numerous veinlets proceeding from the midrib forked, one fork bearing below the summit a superficial sorus of two to five, usually three or four spore-cases. Found in damp rocky forest gullies throughout Queensland, N. S. Wales, Victoria and Tasmania. The small form called G. tenera R. Br. Prod. found in Tasmania differs only from the species in having smaller and more membranous fronds.

G. dichotoma, Hook. This is the largest of the Australian species, fronds dichotomous as the last. Pinnules undivided, linear or linear-lanceolate, on the last branches of the stipes above the last fork, mostly about an inch long but sometimes longer, somewhat stiff, glaucous underneath, dilated and often shortly confluent at the base, the lowest one on the outer side of the rhachis usually longer and more or less pinnatifid. Transverse veinlets proceeding from the midrib branching at the base, one branch bearing near the base a sorus of eight to twelve spore-cases. This fine showy fern is rather plentiful around the borders of tropical scrubs in Queensland and North Australia, it is also said to have been gathered in N. S. Wales. The following note is given in the Flora Australiensis after the description of the species :—" R. Brown in transferring it from Polypodium to Gleichenia rejected Thumberg's specific name as being characteristic of the whole genus and therefore no longer appropriate for a single species. Willdenow nevertheless retained Thumberg's name but placed the plant in Mertensia, now generally united with Gleichenia. Hooker first adopted Thumberg's specific name under Gleichenia and has been followed by most others. The genera in ferns has been thrown into such confusion and uncertainty that pteridologists acknowledge a right of priority in specific names whatever may have been the genus under which they may have been first published."

XI.—Todea, Willd.

Trunk or rhizome erect. Frond compound. Spore-cases globular or nearly so, pedicellate, with a very obscure transverse ring, sometimes only represented by a few parallel striæ near the apex, opening to the base in two valves, clustered in sori on the under surface of the segment. Named in honor of Henry Julius Tode, of Mecklenberg, an eminent Mycologist.

T. barbara, T. Moore. Trunk erect, very thick, from one to six feet high. Frond varying in length from two to eight feet, narrow, stipes slightly angular, naked or at times clothed with brown scales, twice pinnate. Pinnæ numerous from a few inches to a foot long. Pinnules of a firm consistence narrow-lanceolate close one to two inches long, the edge more or less distinctly toothed, the upper ones decurrent and confluent at the base. Sori on the oblique simple or forked veinlets usually covering the greater part of the under surface of the lower pinnules of the lower pinnæ, the rest of the frond barren. Found in swamps or wet places from Rockingham Bay to Moreton Bay in Queensland, also throughout N. S. Wales, Victoria and Tasmania.

T. Fraseri, Hook. et Grev. Trunk or rhizome erect thick. Fronds one to three feet long, twice pinnate. Pinnules lanceolate, dark green and of a thin membranous texture like that of the pellucid species of New Zealand, half to one inch long, deeply serrated. Spore-cases small and few at the base of the midrib and of a few of the lateral veins of the lower pinnules. This species is confined to the deep gullies of the mountains of N. S. Wales.

T. Moorei, Baker. Trunk one to one and a half feet high, six inches diameter. Fronds often four feet long twice pinnate. Pinnules lanceolate of a thin membranous consistence as the last. Spore-cases few and small as in T. Fraseri. So far as at present known this species is confined to Lord Howe's Island.

TRIBE IV.—HYMENOPHYLLEÆ. Fronds of a thin membranous consistence mostly pellucid on usually a creeping rhizome. Spore-cases depressed, with a transverse ring, sessile or nearly so on a columnar receptacle arising from the base of a cup-shaped or deeply two-valved indusium, embedded in or protruding from the margins of the fronds, and of a consistence nearly similar.

XII.—TRICHOMANES, LINN. BRISTLE FERN.

Rhizome creeping, slender, or thick and short, fronds usually small delicate half pellucid, entire or variously divided and veined. Sori terminal or lateral. Indusium (frequently called involucre) of the texture of the frond and continuous with it, tubular or funnel-shaped, entire at the mouth or two lipped, sunk in the margin of the frond, or protruding from it. The receptacle a filiform exserted vein, the spore-cases sessile at its base. Name of uncertain application.

T. peltatum, Baker. Rhizome filiform intricate adhering close to the bark of trees by minute adventitious rootlets. Fronds sessile, orbicular half to one inch broad, attached at or near the centre, overlapping each other and closely appressed entire or broadly lobed, texture very thin and glittering. Veins numerous, free or forked, radiating from the spot where it is attached to the rhizome. Sori few. Indusium tubular more or less embedded in the fronds margin, the mouth sometimes two-lipped, the receptacle scarcely exserted. Found closely clothing the stems of trees in the dense scrubs of the Trinity Bay range.

T. vitiense, Baker. Rhizome filiform, growth similar to last. Fronds shortly stipitate, oblong or linear-cuneate, entire or lobed, one midrib only, no lateral veins four to six lines long. Sori terminal. Indusium tubular embedded in the margin of the frond or scarcely exserted, mouth entire slightly dilated. Receptacle shortly exserted. Found closely adhering to the bark of trees in dense scrubs throughout Queensland.

T. yandinense, Bail. Rhizome filiform densely and intricately matted, clothed more or less with ferruginous hairs. Fronds shortly stipitate, ovate to cuneate, the margins even or repand (slightly uneven) sometimes the apex slightly lobed, four to six lines long. Veins pinnately costæform, with regard to the main division which are prominent, between these are numerous striæform ones also a marginal or intramarginal one to which they all join. Sori terminal usually solitary at the apex of the perfectly ovate fronds, but on some two or three then giving a truncate appearance to the frond. Indusium sunk in the frond, attenuated towards the base, the mouth broad spreading. Receptacle slightly exserted. Found on the logs and trunks of trees in the dense scrubs of Maroochie (Yandina). This beautiful new species forms a connecting link between T. vitiense and T. parvulum having somewhat the form of the former and the veins of the latter.

T. parvulum, Poir. Rhizome filiform, creeping hairy. Fronds stipitate, stipes capillary equal in length to the lamina, usually flabellate but varying in general outline three to five lines in diameter, unequally palmatifid, some of the lobes reaching to near the base, all obtuse or emarginate veins external, in the live plant often of a dark color. Sori terminal. Indusium large for the plant, oblong, tubular spreading at the mouth. Receptacle included or shortly exserted. Found covering the damp rocks, in many parts of Queensland, usually where the scrub is dense as Enoggera Creek near Brisbane, Maroochie, Gympie Road, also in the tropical scrubs.

T. digitatum, Sw. Rhizome filiform creeping hairy. Fronds on a rather long capillary stipes, quarter to half inch long, deeply and unequally divided into three to six broadly linear obtuse entire or notched lobes, bordered by a few small teeth. Indusia broader than in most species, but embedded in the apex of the lobes, with a very short open entire border. Found in Illawarra, N. S. Wales.

T. venosum, R. Br. Rhizome very slender creeping, woolly-scaly. Fronds of the most delicate texture on capillary stipites, two to four inches or even more long pinnate. Pinnules linear or lanceolate, mostly half to one inch long, toothed or with a few short unequal lobes near the base, the veinlets of each pinnule pinnate, with simple or forked branches, the midrib flexuose. Indusium embedded in a short lobe near the base of the pinnule on the inner side, oblong, with a short spreading entire border. Often found on the trunks of tree ferns at the Clarence River and other places in N. S. Wales, the Dandenong Ranges and Victoria, and also many places in Tasmania.

T. javanicum, Blume.   Rhizome creeping.   Fronds lanceolate in outline often falcate, three to four inches long, pinnate. Pinnules numerous crowded along the rhachis, lanceolate-falcate, shortly stipitate, about half inch long, of a thicker consistence and darker color than most species, penniveined, the oblique simple or forked, veinlets mostly produced into short setaceous teeth beyond the margin.   Indusia few, along the inner margin below the middle, wholly exserted, narrow-oblong, with a small spreading border. Receptacle exserted.   Found at the Daintree River, Queensland, so far as at present known its only Australian habitat.

T. rigidum, Sw.   Rhizome erect short thick, stipites tufted dark rough, harsh to the touch.   Fronds ovate-lanceolate or nearly triangular in outline three to six inches long, one and a half to three inches broad at the base, dark and almost coriaceous, bi-pinnate, with deeply pinnatifid lanceolate pinnules and linear dentate segments, the primary and secondary rhachis winged only towards the end.   Indusia very abundant standing in an oblique line from the frond to which they give a bristly appearance, embedded in the lower inner teeth or lobes of the tertiary segment, or sometimes wholly free without any winged margins, narrow, with a small spreading entire border.   Receptacle exserted.   This small dark tufted fern, is one of frequent occurrence near the water's edge of mountain streams in tropical Queensland, also in Southern Queensland and N. S. Wales at the Macleay River, &c.

T. pyxidiferum, Linn.   Rhizome filiform densely matted. Fronds on filiform stipites, seldom more than three inches long, ovate or oblong in outline pinnate.   Pinnæ ovate, deeply pinnatifid or bi-pinnatifid, the lower ones usually distinct, the upper ones connected by a winged rhachis ; lobes few, linear, one nerved.   Indusia occupying nearly the whole of short lateral lobes, often several to each pinnule, oblong, with a broad mouth.   Receptacle either very long or scarcely exserted.   Tropical Queensland, forming large moss-like patches on wet rocks.

T. caudatum, Brack.   Rhizome creeping, rigid, rather stout. Fronds narrow, thin, three to eight inches long, pinnate with pinnatifid pinnæ or bi-pinnate with pinnatifid pinnules, the ultimate segment linear, one-nerved, the upper confluent ones short and rather distinct, giving the pinnules an acuminate aspect.   Indusia half immersed in the short lower inner lobes of the pinnules or segments, shortly oblong, with a narrow spreading border.   Receptacle exserted.   Found at the Tweed River, Illawarra, and several other places in N. S. Wales.

T. apiifolium, Presl.   Rhizome thick and knotty.   Stipes short or long hispid at the base with spreading bristles.   Fronds broadly ovate-lanceolate in outline four to eight inches long bi-pinnate with deeply bi-pinnatifid pinnules.   Primary pinnules one to two inches secondary about half inch long; segments very narrow linear, thin one-nerved. Indusia almost embedded in the short inner lower lobes, the tube shortly turbinate, the border spreading, often rather broad, approaching that of a Hymenophyllum. Found at the Richmond River, New England, and Lord Howe's Island in N. S. Wales.

T. parviflorum, Poir. Rhizome creeping, rather thick. Fronds broadly lanceolate in outline three to .six inches long, bi-pinnate with deeply pinnatifid or pinnate pinnules the segments divided into two to three almost setaceous lobes, giving the whole frond a fennel-like aspect. Indusia the smallest in the genus, not half a line long on little recurved stipites near the base of the pinnules, turbinate, with scarcely spreading border. Queensland habitat Rockingham Bay, York Peninsula.

XIII.—HYMENOPHYLLUM, SM. FILM FERN.

Rhizome slender, creeping, often much branched and matted. Fronds usually small, erect, of a delicate membranous half-pellucid texture, variously divided, the lobes usually linear one-nerved. Sori terminal or lateral. Indusium of the texture of the frond and continuous with it, more or less cup-shaped at the base, and immersed in the margin of the frond, the exserted portion deeply divided into two broad lobes or valves. Receptacle oblong or linear, shorter than the indusium or rarely rather longer. Spore-cases sessile at or near its base. Name from hymen, a membrane, and phyllon, a leaf.

H. marginatum, Hook. et Grev. Fronds on a short filiform stipes half to one inch long, linear and entire or once or twice forked, with central costa and nerve-like margins not toothed. Sori solitary and terminal. Indusium about half line long and broad, divided nearly to the base into obovoid orbicular valves. Port Jackson, N. S. Wales. A rare species.

H. rarum, R. Br. Rhizome creeping filiform. Stipes capillary. Fronds two to four inches long pinnate or deeply pinnatifid; segments or pinnæ once or twice forked, or three or five lobed, or rarely undivided, the upper segments and their lobes confluent with the narrowly winged rhachis, the lowest segments separated by a capillary rhachis; lobes linear, one-nerved, not toothed. Sori terminal. Indusium as broad as the segment, nearly one line diameter, divided to the middle or rather lower into broad rounded valves. Found at Sealer's Cove, Victoria, abundant in Tasmania where it is said to clothe the trunks of tree ferns with a glistening garment of beautiful green.

H. flabellatum, Labill. Rhizome densely matted, rigid. Fronds ovate or lanceolate in outline two to eight inches long, erect or decurved, twice or thrice pinnatifid, the lower segments or pinnæ distant, the rhachis as well as the stipes filiform and not winged, the upper smaller ones confluent with the narrowly winged rhachis, the lobes not dentate. Sori lateral or terminating the smaller lobes. Indusium orbicular or rather broader than long, about half line diameter, deeply divided into entire valves. Found in cool damp places in N. S. Wales and Victoria. Abundant in Tasmania.

H. javanicum, Spreng. Rhizome glabrous creeping. Fronds ovate or lanceolate in outline three to eight inches long, twice or thrice (bi-tripinnatifid) the rhachis winged, with a crisped wing which is continued down the stipes; segments and lobes linear-oblong, obtuse, not dentate. Sori on short lateral lobes, Indusium ovate, about half inch long, divided nearly to the base into entire valves. Found on the Coast Range, Rockingham Bay, in Queensland, Blue Mountains, N. S. Wales, also in a few places in Victoria, but most plentiful in Tasmania.

H minimum, A. Rich. Rhizome filiform, matted. Fronds on short capillary stipes, ovate in outline, quarter to half-inch long, deeply divided into five to eight simple or bifid-segments, slightly denticulate. Sori usually one only to each frond, terminating the main axis. Indusium nearly one line broad, deeply divided into two rounded denticulate open valves. On trees, top of Mount Gower, Lord Howe's Island, N. S. Wales.

H. pumilum, C. Moore. Rhizome filiform, forming broad dense matted patches. Fronds ovate rhomboidal in outline, half to one inch long and nearly as broad, deeply pinnatifid, the pinnæ close together, deeply lobed, the lobes few, broadly linear, with more or less denticulate margins. Sori few, terminating short lobes on the main axis. Indusium about a line in diameter deeply divided into denticulate or rarely entire valves. Found in a few parts of New South Wales.

H. tunbridgense, Sm. Rhizome filiform, much branched and densely matted forming moss-like patches. Fronds numerous on capillary stipites lanceolate in outline, pinnate one to three inches long; pinnæ deeply divided into three to eight linear lobes minutely denticulate on the margin. Sori sessile or on a very short lobe, solitary at the base of the pinnæ on their upper margin. Indusium ovate or orbicular, about one line diameter, divided to much below the middle into more or less denticulate valves. Found on Mount Lindsey, Queensland, and many parts of N. S. Wales, Victoria and Tasmania.

H. multifidum, Swartz. Rhizome creeping matted. Fronds on filiform stipites, rhomboidal in outline, bi-tripinnatifid four inches or more long, the upper segments confluent with the winged rhachis, the lower pinnæ distinct; lobes linear, bordered by minute teeth. Sori usually near the base of the primary or secondary pinnæ on the upper margin as in the last species from which this differs in its compound fronds and in the valves of the indusia being usually entire. Australian habitat; on stems of trees Mount Gower, Lord Howe's Island, N. S. Wales.

TRIBE V. CYATHEÆ.—Trunk arborescent, at least in the Australian species. Fronds large, circinate in vernation, twice or thrice pinnate. Spore-cases numerous, small, with a more or less oblique ring, in globular sori on the under surface of the segments or pinnules.

XIV.—CYATHEA. SMITH.

Tree Ferns, with large twice or thrice pinnate fronds (with regard to Australian species), the transverse veinlets of the pinnules or segments forked or divided, bearing a sorus on one of their branches, the sori arranged in a single row on each side of the mid-rib. Sori globular, enclosed when young in a membranous indusium which after bursting leaves a cup or complete ring under the sorus. Spore-cases numerous, sessile or nearly so on a shortly raised receptacle, each with a vertical or oblique ring. Name derived from the Greek alluding to the small cup-shaped indusium which surrounds the sorus.

C. Lindseyana, Hook.   Caudex or trunk ten to twelve feet high, twelve inches in circumference. Stipes and rhachis unarmed, secondary pinnæ three to four inches long.   Pinnules about half-inch long and two lines broad, the upper ones short and confluent, membranous, glabrous or with a few scaly hairs on the mid-rib, serrulate but not lobed. Sori in a double row near the mid-rib and distant from the margin. Indusium long-persistent, opening with a circular rather small and jagged mouth. Found on Mount Lindsey, Queensland.

C. arachnoidea, Hook. . Trunk fifteen to twenty feet high. Rhachis dark colored, muricated with short black sharp spines and clothed with a close whitish or ferruginous tomentum; fronds tri-pinnate, firm coriaceous glabrous above cobwebby beneath. Secondary pinnæ three to five inches long. Pinnules or segments narrow, the lower ones four to six lines long and distinct, the upper ones smaller and confluent, the fertile portion with recurved crenulated margins. Veins sunk inconspicuous. Sori in a single row on each side of the costule but occupying nearly the whole breadth. Indusia persistent, white, globular, bursting irregularly at the apex. Found among the hills at Rockingham Bay, Queensland.

C. Macarthurii, F. v. M. Trunk ten to twelve feet high, frequently bearing adventitious shoots on its sides. Fronds tripinnate the rhachis covered with a whitish woolly tomentum, which however in some specimens entirely disappears. Secondary pinnæ three to four inches long. Lower pinnules quite distinct though attached by a broad base, three to five lines long, minutely serrate-crenulate, the upper ones gradually smaller and confluent, the pinna ending in a long dentate point. Sori rather small, on the short lateral branches of scarcely prominent forked veinlets, forming a row on each side of the costule. Indusium complete and globular when young, but soon breaking up, leaving a perfect ring under the sorus, or more frequently entirely falling away. Foot of Mount Gower and Lidgebird, Lord Howe's Island, N. S. Wales.

C. medullaris, Sw. Large black tree fern of New Zealand, where it grows to a large size, often thirty feet in height, forming a tree-like trunk of from two to three feet in diameter, the base of which is densely matted with its roots, but the upper part is beautifully marked by the scars from where the fronds have fallen. Fronds ten to fifteen feet long and very broad, tri-pinnate, the rhachis and primary branches sprinkled with small tubercles. Secondary pinnæ four to six inches long, with numerous pinnules, the lower ones distinct, linear, six to nine lines long, crenate or pinnatifid, the upper ones short and confluent into a pinnatifid point. Sori one to each lobe of the pinnule and occupying the greater part of its length. Indusium broad and short under the sorus, irregularly lobed. Found at the Richmond River, N. S. Wales, Cape Otway, Victoria, and near Circular Head, Tasmania.

C. brevipinnæ, Baker. Rhachis, thick, scaly hispid. Primary pinnæ about four inches long and three broad; secondary pinnæ one to one and a half inches long; pinnules three to four lines long, rather broad, entire or slightly lobed at the fruiting parts. Sori large, one to each lobe. At present only known from part of a frond gathered on Lord Howe's Island, N. S. Wales.

XV.—HEMITELIA, R. BR.

Tree ferns, with the habit and principal characters of Cyathea and Alsophila. Sori in the typical American species towards the end of the venules and on all or most of their branches, but in the Australian one and a few others near the base of one fork as in Cyathea. Indusium when open half cup-shaped or semi-circular, interrupted on the upper side and often very deciduous. Name derived from form of indusium.

H. Moorei, Baker. Trunk eight to ten feet high. Fronds tripinnate scaly-hirsute with a ferruginous pubescence often quite disappearing or leaving a few tubercles. Secondary pinnæ lanceolate two to three inches long; pinnules when fertile half inch long, deeply toothed or pinnatifid. Veinlets once forked with a sorus at the base of one fork. Sori thus in a single row on each side of the midrib, one opposite each lobe as in Cyathea, but the indusium when open dimidiate, being quite or almost interrupted on the upper side. Found on side of Mount Gower, on Lord Howe's Island, N. S. Wales.

XVI.—ALSOPHILA, R. BR.

Tree ferns with bi-pinnate fronds, the transverse veinlets of the pinnules or segment forked or divided, bearing a sorus on one or more of their branches. Sori globular, without indusium, but sometimes it is called squamoso-indusiate on account of the scattered scales which are found around the sorus. Spore-cases numerous; sessile or nearly so, usually more or less intermixed with hairs on an elevated receptacle, each with a vertical or oblique

F

ring. The name is derived from alsos, grove, and phileo, to love.
The genus is difficult to distinguish from Polypodium, the raised
receptacle is perhaps the best characteristic mark but the tree-like
habit of all Australian species is another distinguishing mark.

A. Rebeccæ, F. v. M.   Trunk slender dark colored six to nine
feet high, often forming a thick mass of shoots at their base. Main
rhachis of frond dark rough.   Secondary pinnæ dark and shining,
undivided lanceolate, two to three inches long, four to five lines broad
or rather more when barren, acuminate, crenate or obtusely serrate,
obliquely truncate at the base but not adnate to the rhachis.
Transverse veinlets with three to seven branches.   Sori rather
large, on two to four of the branches, forming about two irregular
rows on each side of the midrib.   Found in the close rocky gullies
of the Rockingham Bay Range, Daintree River, Port Denison, and
Cape York Peninsula.

A. Loddigessii, Kunge.   Secondary pinnæ two to three inches
long lanceolate, deeply pinnatifid the segments all confluent at the
base, more ovate than in A. Australis, three to four lines long, two
to two and a half lines broad, obtuse or almost acute, entire; transverse veinlets entire or once forked.   Sori rather small, one to four
on each side of the costule of each segment.   Found at Cape
Byron, N. S. Wales.

A. Australis, R. Br.   Trunk ten to thirty feet high, stout often
covered with the bases of the old fronds.   Frond bi-tripinnate six
to twelve feet long, three to four feet broad, stipes, and whole frond
in a young state, densely clothed with linear-lanceolate and setaceous
pale colored scales, the stipes, main rhachis and sometimes the
secondary ones muricate.   Secondary pinnæ three to five feet long;
pinnules lanceolate or linear, the lower ones distinct and four to six
lines long, the upper ones shorter and confluent, the soriferous part
entire or obscurely crenate, the barren one and the barren end of the
soriferous ones often serrulate.   Transverse veinlets usually once
forked when soriferous, often with three to four branches when
barren.   Sori in two rows sometimes extending to the apex and as
many as eight on each side of the costule, often fewer extending
half way or reduced to very few at the base of the segment.   In
this species is merged A. excelsa, R. Br. which certainly does not
differ enough to form a good variety.   This handsome tree fern
is the most widely spread of all the Australian kinds, being
found throughout Southern Queensland, and also in several
tropical parts.   Common also in N. S. Wales, Victoria and
Tasmania.

A. Leichhardtiana, F. v. M.   Prickly tree Fern.   Trunk ten to
twenty feet high, slender hard and dark, very different in general
appearance from any others of the genus.   Frond large spreading
the rhachis dark rough or mucronate-spinulose, sometimes slightly
tomentose, secondary pinnæ oblong acuminate, sessile, pinnatifid
at the apex the lower pinnules detached and serrate.   Sori in very

distinct series close to costula. Found most abundant in Queensland in the Maroochie scrubs, but also met with in many parts of N. S. Wales.

A. Robertsiana, F. v. M. Trunk six to eight feet high, not thick. Fronds bi-pinnate, the rhachis both general and partial as well as the pinnules and sori hispid or sprinkled with rigid hairs. Secondary pinnæ two to three inches long. Pinnules distinct, four to six lines long, deeply pinnatifid, the upper ones of each pinnæ smaller more entire and confluent. Sori rather large, solitary opposite each lobe of the pinnule. Found in the deep close gullies of the Ranges, Rockingham Bay, Queensland.

TRIBE VI. POLYPODIEÆ.—Habit various. Spore-cases small, with a longitudinal or scarcely oblique ring, usually bursting on one side in the shape of little helmets, numerous and stipitate in sori or patches on the under side or rarely on the margins of the fronds, with or without an indusium.

A Sori covered at least when young with an indusium.

XVII.—DICKSONIA, L'HERITIER.

Trunk arborescent, or a creeping rhizome. Fronds large, compound. Pinnules penniveined. Sori terminating veins close to the margins of the frond. Indusium either globular and two-valved or cup-shaped and entire, the upper valve or upper part of the cup adnate to the frond, and continuous with the margin. Name in honor of Mr. James Dickson, a Scotch botanist.

D. antarctica, Labill. Woolly-tree fern. Trunk or candex said to attain thirty to fifty feet in height with a diameter of four feet at the base, always much stouter in the stem than the other Australian tree ferns. Fronds six to twelve feet long, bitripinnate,.the stipes and rhachis scabrous or smooth, covered with soft hair in a young state. Secondary pinnæ two to three inches long. Pinnules or segments distinct or the upper ones confluent, nearly flat and acutely toothed when barren, thicker and obtusely lobed when fertile. Sori solitary on each lobe. Indusium globular, about half line diameter two-valved, the upper valve adnate to the lobe of the frond and undistinguishable from it except near the base where there is on each side a narrow free margin. Only met with in quite the southern parts of Queensland, but generally throughout N. S. Wales, Victoria and Tasmania, as also in a few parts of South Australia.

D. Youngiæ, C. Moore. Trunk ten to twelve feet high, marked by scars showing the junction of the former fronds with the caudex. Fronds more coriaceous and glossy than in D. antarctica. Stipes clothed with rather long glossy brown hair ; rhachis ferruginous-pubescent or glabrous, not scabrous. Secondary pinnæ two to three inches long. Pinnules three to six lines long when fertile, deeply divided into rounded lobes like those of the last species but larger. Indusium one line diameter, the upper valve entirely adnate.

Found on the Bunya Mountains and Bellender Ker Range in Queensland ; at the Richmond River, Tweed River and New England in N. S. Wales. I have not received any fertile specimens of the tree-fern which Mr. W. Hill brought a short time ago from Fraser's Island, but from the sterile state of one of the plants in the Botanic Gardens, Brisbane, it seems to connect D. Youngiæ with D. squarrosa, Sw. of New Zealand.

D. davallioides, R. Br.   Rhizome long creeping.   Stipes chestnut brown, glossy slightly hairy.   Frond membranous, flaccid, somewhat hairy, decompound.   Secondary pinnæ three to four inches long.   Pinnules numerous, distinct, half to one inch long, pinnatifid, the lowest lobe on the upper side longer than the others. Sori small, globular, almost marginal in the sinus or at the base of the upper side of the lobes of the pinnules.   Indusium cupular (cup-shaped), about half line diameter, entire or scarcely lobed, adnate on the upper side to the frond.   This delicate and beautiful fern grows in great profusion along the sides of many Queensland Creeks, but seems more generally met with in N. S. Wales, also at Cape Otway, Victoria.

XVIII.—DEPARIA, HOOK. ET GREV.

Rhizome creeping.   Fronds large, compound.   Sori globular, terminating a vein, protruding from the margin of the frond and sometimes stipitate beyond it.   Indusium membranous, shortly and broadly cup-shaped or two-valved.   Name from depas, a cup, form of involucre, or indusium.

D. prolifera, Hook.   Fronds two to three feet long, pinnate. Lower pinnæ six inches to one foot long, deeply pinnatifid ; segments ovate or oblong, somewhat falcate, quarter to half-inch long, all connected by a winged rhachis two to three lines broad, sori sessile upon the margin of the frond.

D. nephrodioides, Baker.   Rhizome creeping.   Fronds two to three feet high, rather firm and shining, twice or thrice pinnate. Secondary pinnæ two to three inches long, pinnate or deeply pin- natifid ; lower pinnules pinnatifid half to one inch long, upper ones gradually smaller confluent and toothed only.   Sori marginal and prominent but sessile, globose.   Indusium very shortly and broadly divided into two valves, partly formed by a slight dilatation or obtuse tooth of the frond.   Saddle, between Mount Gower and Lidgebird, Lord Howe's Island, New South Wales.

XIX.—DAVALLIA, SM.

Rhizome creeping, often densely covered with soft scales or setæ. Fronds compound, often large, or rarely in species not Australian undivided.   Sori globular or slightly elongated, terminating veins close under or at a little distance from the margin.   Indusium from under the sorus either with the margins adnate to the frond and forming with it a complete cup enclosing the sorus, or attached only by its broad base, and either covering the sorus or short and open under it. Name in honor of Edward Davall, a Swiss botanist.

D. solida, Swartz. Rhizome rather thick, densely clothed with setose appressed scales. Fronds one to two feet long, rather broad, bi-tripinnate or pinnatifid. Pinnules coriaceous, half to one and half inches long, the lower larger ones distinct and deeply pinnatifid, the upper ones confluent and obtusely lobed. Sori at the base of the crenatures or lobes. Indusium narrow, oblong, three-quarter line long, the margins adnate, forming with the frond a complete cup or tube. The only Australian habitat noticed Hummocky Island, Queensland.

D. elegans, Sw. Rhizome densely clothed with soft light colored scales, creeping in the loose sandy soil around coast swamps. Fronds decompound, one to three feet high, the pinnæ often tapering into long points. Pinnules lanceolate, deeply pinnatifid, coriaceous, smooth shining and elegantly marked with raised striæ distinct from the veins. Sori on small truncate or bi-dentate lobes or teeth. Indusium ovate, about half-line long and broad, the margins adnate and forming with the tube a complete cup, which is of a silvery whiteness. Found at various places along the Queensland tropical coast.

D. pyxidata, Cav. Hare's foot fern. Rhizome thick, densely clothed with soft brown scales. Fronds one to two feet long coriaceous, deltoides-ovate, on a stipes about half as long, bi-tripinnate. Pinnules smooth and shining, the lobes or segments mostly obtuse. Sori on the lobes or teeth. Indusium ovate, sometimes broad, but more frequently narrow and truncated at the mouth. This beautiful fern is usually met with growing in the large masses formed by the stag's-horn and bird's-nest ferns or in the cracks of trees or old logs throughout Queensland and New South Wales.

D. pedata, Sm. Rhizome long creeping, scaly, forming dense masses on rocks, giving them the appearance of being covered with ivy. From the dark green coriaceous fronds which are ovate-triangular from two to four inches long, the stipes short or of equal length, deeply pinnatifid, the lowest pair of segments usually again pinnatifid and deeply so on the outer side, the others gradually smaller and entire or scarcely crenate, obtuse or truncate. Sori at the base of the crenatures at the end or upper half of the segments. Indusium nearly orbicular, about half line diameter, closely appressed and covering the sorus but attached only by the broad base, leaving the margins free. Found covering rocks in wet gullies of tropical Queensland.

D. dubia, R. Br. Mountain bracken. Rhizome horizontal stout, Fronds large subcoriaceous, tri-pinnate, three to six feet high. Pinnules half to one and half inches long, lanceolate, deeply pinnatifid and the lowest segments often again toothed or lobed. Sori at the base of the obtuse teeth or lobes which are often curved over them as in Dicksonia, but quite independent of them. Indu-

sium about quarter line broad and very short, thus scarcely discernible
when the sorus is ripe, attached only by the broad base, often hairy.
This fern is found abundant in Queensland, both north and south,
growing on the side of creeks and damp hills; it is also plentiful
in N. S. Wales, Victoria and Tasmania. In many good works on
ferns this species is spoken of as resembling Dicksonia davallioides,
but in Queensland where the two are found in company they differ
nearly as much in general appearance as the two Todeas T. barbara
and T. hymenophylloides.

D. speluncæ, Baker. Rhizome creeping. Fronds large, flaccid,
bi-tripinnate. Secondary pinnæ lanceolate, two to four inches long,
pinnate in the lower part, pinnatifid towards the end, membranous,
hairy underneath as well as the rhachis. Lower pinnules half to
three-quarter inch long, pinnatifid, the upper ones gradually smaller
and confluent, reduced towards the end to small lobes. Sori
several on each pinnule below the sinus of the lobes, forming two
rows at same distance from the margin. Indusium broad short,
membranous, slightly toothed or jagged, attached only by the broad
base. Found in several parts of tropical Queensland.

D. tripinnata, F. v. M. This is said to be an elegant fern and
confined so far as at present known to the Bellender Ker Range,
Queensland. The following is the discription given in the Flora
Australiensis of a single frond eight inches long, six inches broad
at the base, stipes hairy six inches long, thrice pinnate, the main
rhachis hairy. Primary pinnæ lanceolate, secondary oblong half to
one inch long, pinnules two to four lines, deeply divided into two to
four obovate obtuse lobes, dark green on both sides but rather thin,
the lower pinnæ and pinnules quite distinct, the upper ones smaller
and confluent at the base. Sori few in the specimen under the
sinus of some of the smaller lobes. Indusium membranous, broad
and somewhat jagged, attached only by the broad base.

XX.—Vittaria, Sm.

Rhizome creeping. Fronds simple, linear, the veins oblique
connected by an intramarginal veins. Sori continuous lying in a
groove at or near the margin, the substance of the frond forming
a two-valved indusium. Name derived from vitta, a ribbon,
referring to the drooping fronds.

V. elongata, Swartz. Grass-leaved fern. Rhizome shortly
creeping covered with dark colored hair-like scales. Frond varying
in length from a few inches to several feet, and with a breadth of
from one to five lines, acute, or obtuse at the end, gradually tapering
into a short dark colored stipes of a rather coriaceous texture.
Veins very oblique, sometimes almost parallel with the costa. Sori
usually extending nearly the whole length of the frond. This
curious grass-like fern may be frequently seen fringing the stems of
the tree in the scrubs of tropical Queensland, in which situation the
fronds are usually very long. At Maroochie, a place about eighty miles

from Brisbane, it is also plentiful on the trunks of trees but here the fronds are much shorter. It has also been met with in N. S. Wales at the Richmond and Macleay River scrubs.

XXI.—LINDSÆA, DRYANDER.

Rhizome creeping or shortly horizontal. Fronds pinnate or compound undivided in some species (not Australian). Sori in a continuous or interrupted line under the margin of the frond, with a continuous indusium opening along the upper or outer margin, the margin of the frond sometimes slightly dilated and assuming the appearance of an upper valve. Veins forked, free or anastomosing. Named in honor of Mr. John Lindsay, author of Observations on the Germination of Ferns.

L. linearis, Sw. Rhizome creeping, scales brittle. Fronds pinnate, very fragile, linear, stipes and rhachis usually glossy black from a few inches to over one foot high. Pinnæ sessile flabellate, obliquely cuneate or almost dimidiate three to four lines broad. Sori forming a continuous line under the outer margin. Queensland habitat Moreton Bay, Eight-mile Plains, common in crevices of rocks, Stanthorpe. N. S. Wales, Port Jackson, Blue Mountains, New England and Hastings River. In Victoria this plant is said to be plentiful in the dry forests of the Western districts, also in Gippsland. Abundant in heathy places in Tasmania. Onkaparinga River, South Australia, and is one of the few ferns found in Western Australia.

L. dimorpha, Bail. Queensland Ferns. Rhizome a tufted knot, densely clothed with bright glossy golden scales. Fronds usually numerous in a close tuft, pinnate, sterile ones two to three inches high, with broad flabellate pinnæ lobed with short obtuse lobes. Fertile fronds much longer, the stipes and rhachis slender and pale colored, pinnæ broad and short divided to the base bipartite, reflexed, the broad tops touching each other giving a lunate appearance to the pinna. Sori broad lobed. Queensland, Eight-mile Plains, Kedron Brook, and near the top of one of the Glasshouse Mountains.

L. cultrata, Sw. Rhizome tufted or very shortly creeping. Fronds pinnate three to six inches long, tufted stipes and rhachis slender pale colored. Pinnæ near together in the upper part of the frond the lowest pair often distant, very oblique or half-reniform, three to four lines broad, the rounded outer margin entire, with the sorus and indusium continuous or slightly lobed or denticulate interrupting the sori. Common on damp rocks in Northern Queensland, also found on the rocks about Maroochie.

L. flabellulata, Dryand. Rhizome creeping. Fronds six to twelve inches high, usually bipinnate two or more of the lower pinnæ being again pinnate and two to four inches long, the upper pinnæ entire, but sometimes the whole frond simply pinnate or in other specimens more or less tripinnate. Pinnules oblique in the simply pinnate part flabellate or almost rhomboid often half inch broad, smaller in the more compound specimens. Veins forked, free or very rarely here and there anastomosing. Sori continuous round the margin or interrupted. On rocks of most of the ranges of Northern Queensland.

L. lobata, Poir. Rhizome creeping. Fronds six to twelve inches high, simply pinnate or bipinnate with few pinnate pinnæ at the base, much resembling the less-branched forms of L. flabellulata but the fertile pinnæ often more than half inch broad, and the veinlets frequently anastomosing. Northern Queensland damp rocks.

L. trichomanoides, Dryand. Rhizome closely knotted, or very shortly creeping. Fronds rather rigid six to twelve inches high, bipinnate. Primary pinnæ almost opposite, usually half inch long, pinnules obovate or oblong-cuneate, equilateral, two to three lines long, the upper ones confluent, all rounded and entire at the end with a continuous sorus, or notched with an interrupted sorus and indusium. Veinlets forked, not anastomosing. Found near Mac-quarrie Harbour, Tasmania, and perhaps at a few places in N. S. Wales, but uncertain.

L. microphylla, Sw. Rhizome closely knotted or shortly creeping and densely clothed with glossy brown scales. Fronds six to eighteen inches high, bi-tripinnate, elongated or oblong-lanceolate in outline, stipites hairy at the base, rhachis flexuose. Primary pinnæ distant, barren pinnules varying from ovate to lanceolate, toothed or lobed ; fertile ones obovate, cuneate or flabellate, equi-lateral, one to two or more lines broad, undivided with a continuous sorus, or notched or lobed with the sori interrupted. In Queensland near Brisbane, common along Stony Creek, also on hill-sides under a good shade. Also Port Jackson, Clarence River and New Eng-land, N. S. Wales.

L. incisa, Prentice. Rhizome long creeping, of a bright golden color, sparsely clothed with hair-like white scales, often forked, fronds from its whole length, often close four or six to the inch. Fronds from a few inches to two feet long, pinnate, pinnæ occupying nearly the whole length of frond, stipes and rhachis, tetragonous. Pinnæ entire flabelliform, bi-trifid or divided into three or more bifid cuneate pinnules. Sori large, with a deep, entire or notched indusium. Queensland : usually found on damp sandy soil under the shade of small trees, Eight-mile Plains, Brisbane River, &c.

L. Fraseri, Hook. Rhizome long creeping wiry. Fronds pinnate six to eighteen inches high, stipites short. Pinnæ membranous, distant ; from ovate to lanceolate, equilateral, obtuse, truncate or cordate at the base and shortly petiolate, quarter to one inch long, the upper ones smaller and somewhat rhomboidal, the barren ones often denticulate, the veinlets frequently anastomosing. Sori marginal continuous or slightly interrupted. Common in swamps at the Glasshouse Mountains, Moreton Bay, Eight-mile Plains and other parts of Southern Queensland.

L. ensifolia, Sw. Rhizome creeping. Fronds simply pinnate

and six to eighteen inches high in some forms, while others are variously divided, bi-pinnate or having elongated pinnatifid pinnæ with numerous small segments. Pinnæ or pinnules exceedingly variable in number and shape, ovate obovate, linear or lanceolate, one to three inches long, barren ones often serrulate, the frond often ending in a long ensiform lobe. Veins more or less anastomosing. Sori continuous along the whole margin except the short equally cuneate base. All the various forms may be found on the same rhizome so it is impossible to make marked varieties. And perhaps it would be advisable to include L. Fraseri as a variety of this species, as the lower pinnæ of that species are frequently deeply lobed. Common along the borders of swamps throughout North Australia and the whole of Queensland.

L. lanuginosa, Wall. Rhizome stout creeping, epiphytical. Frond one to four feet long, pinnate with the rhachis densely woolly tomentose, the old fronds becoming glabrous. Pinnæ numerous, coriaceous, more or less falcate, obtuse or acute, very deciduous. Veins simple or forked, diverging from the costule all free, a white dot on the upper side marking where they terminate just within the margin. Sori continuous along the margins except the obliquely truncate base. Found forming immense masses on the trees of North Queensland scrubs. Although a most beautiful fern seldom seen in cultivation.

XXII.—ADIANTUM, LINN.   MAIDEN-HAIR FERN.

Rhizome creeping or tufted. Frond simple or compound. Pinnules more or less petiolate, often oblique. Veins forked or dichotomous radiating from the petiolule to the margin without any mid-rib. Sori marginal, short and distinct or partly elongated and confluent. Indusium continuous with the margin and recurved bearing the spore-cases on its under surface. Name derived from the Greek Adiantos, in allusion to the dry texture of their fronds or perhaps on account of their possessing in a remarkable degree the property of repelling water.

A. lunulatum, Burm. Rhizome short. Fronds tufted, pinnate, six to twelve inches long, the rhachis extended beyond the pinnæ and proliferous. Pinnæ articulated on slender petiolules of one to four lines, obliquely fan-shaped, half to one inch or more broad. Sori elongated, sometimes continuous along the whole outer margin, but often more or less interrupted. Port Darwin in North Australia, and Rockingham Bay in Queensland.

A. capillus-veneris, Linn. Maiden-hair of England. Rhizome creeping. Fronds bi-pinnate, broadly ovate in outline, six to twelve inches long and sometimes nearly as broad, the rhachis capillare. Pinnules on short petiolules, broadly obovate or obliquely flabelli-form, four to eight lines broad, more or less divided into cuneate, obtuse or truncate lobes, thin, of a bright green. Sori at the end

G

of most of the lobes and usually occupying their whole breadth. Said to have been collected on the wet rocks near Rockhampton.

A. æthiopicum, Linn.   Small Maiden-hair fern.   Rhizome tufted or stoloniferous.   Fronds from a few inches to one and half feet high, and sometimes very broad, two to four pinnate, the rhachis slender shining, often flexuose.   Pinnules on short often capillare petiolules, mostly obovate-orbicular with a more or less cuneate equal base, three to five lines broad, thin and bright green, broadly crenate or shortly lobed.   Sori distinct in the sinus of the crenatures, the reflexed indusium reniform or at length transversely oblong.   Common throughout Australia reaching into the interior and also in Tasmania.

A. formosum, R. Br.   Tall scrub Maiden-hair fern.   Rhizome creeping, scaly, often deep in the soil.   Fronds one to four feet high, broadly spreading two to four pinnate, the stipes often scabrous usually black with numerous pinnæ, the primary and secondary ones always simply pinnate at the end, the main rhachis usually flexuose, slender and black.   Pinnules membranous or scarcely coriaceous, shortly petiolulate, obliquely obovate or rhomboidal, usually three to four lines long, the entire sides very unequal, the upper margin when barren crenate.   Sori on or between the teeth. Indusium somewhat reniform.   Very abundant throughout Queensland in dense scrubs, also plentiful in N. S Wales and Tasmania.

A. affine, Willd.   Rhizome long, creeping over rocks and often exposed.   Fronds very spreading, sparsely divided on tall black stipites one to two feet high, bi-tripinnate.   Pinnule nearly sessile, very obliquely ovate or oblong-rhomboidal four to eight lines broad, the under surface often of a light color, outer margins dentate. Sori marginal, scarcely indented.   Indusium broadly reniform. Found creeping over the rocks in the water courses at Maroochie in Queensland; also at Port Jackson, Blue Mountains and Richmond and Macleay rivers, N. S. Wales.   Var. intermedium is a form in which the indusium differs somewhat, resembling more that of A. formosum and has been collected both in Queensland and N. S. Wales.

A. diaphanum, Blume.   Rhizome tufted.   Fronds six to twelve inches high, stipes slender the two to five upper pinnæ three to six inches long, the lower ones sometimes with one or two secondary ones at the base.   Pinnules numerous, very shortly stalked, obliquely ovate-rhomboidal very unequal at the base, thinly membranous, three to six lines broad, the outer margin dentate.   Sori in the sinus of the teeth.   Indusium deeply reniform.   Queensland, Rockingham Bay, Daintree River in the north, and at or near the southern border, also Richmond River in N. S. Wales.

A. hispidulum, Sw.   Rough stalked Maiden-hair fern.   Rhizome tufted.   Fronds once or twice forked at the base, each branch ending in a long falcate pinnæ or pinnately divided at the base or higher up into secondary pinnæ.   Pinnules very numerous, on short petiolules, obliquely ovate-rhomboid, three to eight lines long or broad, rather rigid, prominently veined, the under surface as well as the rhachis usually hispid ; the young fronds usually of a purplish color. Sori usually almost contiguous though not confluent. Indusia much recurved, orbicular slightly reniform. Common throughout Queensland and N. S. Wales, also Genoa River, Victoria.

XXIII.—HYPOLEPIS, BERNH.

Rhizome creeping. Fronds compound, usually large, the pinnules penniveined. Sori marginal, short in the sinus of the teeth of the pinnules. Indusium a small scale continuous with the margin, recurved over the sorus, the spore-cases attached at its base. Name from hypo, beneath, and lepis a scale, referring to position of sorus.

H. tenuifolia, Bernh. Rhizome long, clothed with dense white hairs. Fronds four to seven feet high including the long hairy, stout stipes, and often two feet broad, tri-quadripinnate ; primary pinnæ or branches spreading ; secondary and tertiary narrow, linear or oblong one and a half to two inches long, deeply pinnatifid. Lobes linear-oblong, blunt, bluntly crenate. Sori few or several to each segment in the sinus of the teeth, the reflexed scale-like indusium at first often covering the sorus but in an advanced stage almost concealed under the sorus or quite withered away. The plant usually covered with glandular hairs. Found on the borders of scrubs throughout Queensland and N. S. Wales. I have a portion of a frond from Gippsland which seems rather to belong to this plant than Polypodium punctatum with which it is sometimes confused.

XXIV.—CHEILANTHES, SW.

Rhizome tufted or creeping. Fronds usually small, twice or thrice pinnate with small lobed segments. Sori globular and distinct at the end of the veinlets or oblong by the confluence of two or more, all marginal, the slightly altered teeth or lobes bent over them and forming an indusium with the spore-cases inserted at their base as in Pteris. Veinlets forked from a central nerve. Name from cheilos, a lip, and anthos a flower ; from the form of the indusium.

C. tenuifolia, Sw. Curly fern. Rhizome knotty or shortly horizontal. Fronds cæspitose from a few inches to over one foot high, broadly ovate triangular in outline, the stipes and main rhachis red-brown glabrous or with a few hairs. Primary pinnæ nearly opposite in distant pairs, often a few inches long and broad, elegantly pinnate a second or a third time, the tertiary pinnules deeply pinnatifid, the ultimate segments in all cases ovate or oblong obtuse one to four lines long. Sori numerous round the margins, nearly contiguous, with the small rounded teeth or lobes bent over them. Widely distributed over the Australian Colonies and Tasmania.

Var. Sieberi. Rhizome short, almost erect. Fronds tufted, erect, oblong in outline, from a few inches to one and a half feet high, and one to three inches broad, sori punctiform often very dark. The most common form in southern Queensland.

Var. nudiuscula. Rhizome short. Fronds tufted near the form of V. Sieberi, but of a more coriaceous texture and densely pubescent. Sori broader and more of a brown color. Found usually on the borders of creeks in tropical Queensland.

C. caudata, R. Br. Supposed to be only another variety of C. tenuifolia, but little known at present. Frond six to eight inches long, slender, bipinnate at least at the base, the pinnæ not numerous, all, whether primary or secondary, ending in a narrow-linear pinnule, usually at least half an inch long, continuous or interrupted at the base, and soriferous throughout, the few segments at the base of the pinnæ shortly linear. Endeavour River, Port Bowen and Gilbert River, Queensland.

XXV.—PTERIS, LINNÆUS.

Rhizome creeping, or short thick and erect, or horizontal. Fronds usually large and compound rarely small or simple. Veins simple forked or anastomosing, with or without a midrib. Sori linear, continuous or slightly interrupted along the margin of the segment with a continuous narrow membranous indusium proceeding from the margin and opening along the inner or lower edge. Spore-cases inserted on the frond under the indusium. Name derived from the Greek pteryx, a wing, or pteron, a feather, alluding to the graceful feather like fronds of some species.

P. geraniifolia, Raddi. Rhizome tufted. Fronds broadly rounded cordate in outline, two to four inches long and broad coriaceous, tripartite, the lateral divisions divaricate, all deeply pinnatifid, the lower segments again pinnatifid, the upper ones short and entire; lobes all obtusely lanceolate or ovate, stipes and principal veins black, the latter forked but mostly concealed in the substance of the frond. Sori continuous on the lobes. Met with in various parts of tropical Queensland, also in the swamps off the Brisbane River; and New England, N. S. Wales.

P. paradoxa, Baker. Rhizome shortly creeping. Fronds six to eighteen inches high, pinnate, stipes dark clothed with appressed narrow scales. Pinnæ often on young plants of this and the next species only one and that more or less cordate. On the larger fronds five to eleven or more, shortly petiolulate, ovate lanceolate, one and a half to three inches long, the terminal one often lobed, coriaceous, dull green above, often glaucous beneath. Veins free dichotomous, oblique from the midrib but mostly concealed in the substance of the frond. Sori very broad continuous all round the pinnæ. Indusium not so thin as in some species, soon concealed under the sori. Common in south Queensland scrubs, and a few of the more northern. Also in New England, Port Jackson, Richmond and Tweed River scrubs, N. S. Wales.

P. falcata, R. Br. Ear fern. Rhizome creeping. Fronds six inches to two feet long, pinnate, the stipes and rhachis densely scaly-hirsute, Pinnæ numerous, distant, nearly sessile, lanceolate, usually falcate, one to two inches long, rather obtuse, cariaceous with the venation concealed, the lower ones at times auriculate at the base on the upper side, and usually at a much greater distance apart. Sori very broad, occupying nearly half the width of pinna, continuous all round except near the apex, and the truncate base. Found in parts of New South Wales, near Melbourne, at the Grampians, and near Sale, Gippsland, and Tasmania.

Var. nana. Rhizome very short. Fronds tufted, pinnæ much closer almost overlapping, much smaller and more acute than in the species, often over eighty on a frond of eighteen inches long. This is the form mostly met with in Queensland, and common in every scrub, on rocks, logs, &c.

Var. rotundifolia. This has the same habit as the species differing only in form of pinnæ which is more orbicular. It is said to have been gathered on Mount Dryander, and Mount Lindsey, in Queensland. I cannot find any character by which to separate this last form, the Pellæa rotundifolia of Hooker's species Filicum from P. falcata, and think also it would have been better to have followed Baron Mueller and have included as another form P. paradoxa.

P. longifolia, Linn. Rhizome short and thick. Fronds one to three feet high, pinnate, lanceolate in outline, stipes hairy-scaly at the base. Pinnæ numerous, nearly sessile, linear or linear-lanceolate, three to six inches long; veins simple or forked, transverse from the costule. Sori continuous along the whole margin except the small rounded, cordate, or truncate base. Found in Queensland near Brisbane, also on the main range, and a few places in the tropics; in N. S. Wales, Blue Mountains, New England, &c., and in Gippsland, Victoria.

P. ensiformis, Burm. Rhizome short, scaly. Fronds nine to eighteen inches high, pinnate, stipes long, glabrous. Pinnæ when fertile narrow linear, entire, lobed or again pinnate at the base. terminal lobe the longest, often over four inches long, the lateral ones often shortly decurrent; lobes of the barren fronds sometimes ovate and denticulate; veins forked, transverse from the costule. Sori continuous round the fertile lobes. Queensland, Herbert River, Endeavour River, Cape York Peninsula, Port Denison. A pretty little fern of easy culture.

P. umbrosa, R. Br. Rhizome short, knotted somewhat erect. Fronds one to three feet high, pinnate, the stipes often slightly rough. Pinnæ thirteen or more linear-lanceolate, four to nine inches long, entire or the lower ones again divided into three to five similar segments, all more or less decurrent on the rhachis, usually broader and minutely serrulate when barren, and the barren ends of fertile ones often deeply serrate; veinlets transverse, mostly forked. Sori continuous down the decurrent base. Taylor's

46   THE FERN WORLD OF AUSTRALIA.

Range and various parts of Main Range, Queensland; also in
numerous places in N. S. Wales, and at the Genoa, Victoria.

P. quadriaurita, Retz.   Rhizome short erect.   Fronds pinnate,
one to three feet high.   Pinnæ mostly opposite, four to eight inches
long, regularly and deeply pinnatifid, otherwise undivided, or the
lower ones with one or two similar secondary pinnæ on the lower
side.   Pinnules or segments numerous, broadly linear, often falcate,
obtuse, four to eight lines long, confluent at the base, the pinnæ
usually ending in a long linear-lanceolate point lobed at the base.
Sori often not reaching the base of the segment.   Common on the
ranges of tropical Queensland.

P. tremula, R. Br.   Rhizome short, thick, erect.   Fronds two
to six feet high, erect, glabrous, twice or four times pinnate, usually
of a delicate texture, pinnæ nearly opposite.   Stipites and rhachis
often of a rich chestnut brown.   Ultimate segments linear, rather firm
when in fruit, quarter to one inch long, slightly decurrent, membranous flat and serrulate when barren; veins mostly forked and
transverse.   Sori usually continuous but scarcely reaching the base
of the segments and sometimes interrupted, at length expanded so
as to conceal the indusium.   Found on the borders of scrubs in
many parts of Queensland, N. S. Wales, Victoria and Tasmania.

P. aquilina, Linn.   The common bracken var. esculenta is the
form found in Australia.   Rhizome long thick and creeping, often
some distance beneath the surface.   Fronds rather tall or short,
according to quality of soil, mostly tri-pinnate.   Primary pinnæ
distant, the lowest pair much larger and more compound than the
rest, which gradually decrease to the apex of frond, thus giving it
a somewhat triangular outline, at times four feet broad.   Secondary
or tertiary pinnæ numerous, lanceolate, deeply pinnatifid or pinnate,
always ending in a linear undivided obtuse segment, the lateral
segments oblong or linear, scarcely widened at the base, but decurrent on the rhachis, the costule usually raised, dilated and
hardened with acute ciliate edges and the under surface usually
hairy between the costule and the sori.   Sori continuous along the
margin, the rather broad indusium really marginal, but the frond
thickened and often minutely crenulate at the base of the indusium
make it appear intramarginal.   Common and abundant in all the
colonies.

P. incisa, Thunb.   Bat's-wing fern.   Rhizome long creeping.
Frond one to six feet high, on stout stipites which near the base
are often muricated, of a rich brown, often glaucous, bi-tripinnate.
Pinnules of the barren fronds usually deeply pinnatifid, one to two
inches long, with broad obtuse membranous lobes, the veins proceeding from the mid-rib of the pinnule, repeatedly forked in each
lobe, the branches here and there anastomosing or all free.   In the
fertile frond the secondary pinnæ often pinnate at the base, pinnatifid
in the upper part, the lower pinnules or segments with a distinct
mid-rib and variously branched veins, the upper lobes less regularly
veined.   Sori continuous or interrupted, often neither reaching the

base nor the apex of the segment. Frequently met with on hill-sides or ranges of Southern Queensland, banks of Brisbane River, &c.; also in similar places in N. S. Wales, Victoria and Tasmania; rare in South Australia.

P. marginata, Bory. Rhizome very thick, short and erect. Fronds having very stout stipites several feet in height, the main rhachis branched, usually tri-partite, each branch pinnate. Pinnæ numerous, three to ten inches long, deeply pinnatifid; segments oblong or broadly linear, often falcate, obtuse, quarter to one inch long, confluent into a winged rhachis two to three lines broad; veins copiously anastomosing on each side of the mid-rib. Sori often continued round the sinus, but rarely reaching the ends of the lobes. Barren fronds thinner, the lobes often minutely dentate. One of the handsomest of all the Queensland ferns, generally met with in the tropical scrubs.

P. comans, Forst. This fern is said to be near P. marginata but more branched. Secondary pinnæ four to ten inches long, deeply pinnatifid; segments numerous, half to two inches long, oblong-lanceolate or linear, often falcate, decurrent along the rhachis which is not, however, uniformly winged as in P. marginata; some of the lower segments sometimes again shortly pinnatifid; veins copiously reticulate. Sori usually continued round the sinus, but rarely to the tips of the lobes. Barren segments or barren tips of the fertile ones usually dentate. South Queensland, N. S. Wales, Victoria and Tasmania.

XXIV.—LOMARIA, WILLD.

Rhizome creeping, or in some caudiciform. Fronds pinnate, pinnatifid or entire; the first of each year's growth usually barren, the inner fertile ones with linear pinnules, sometimes a few sterile abbreviated pinnæ or lobes at the base of fertile frond. Sori in a continuous line on each side of the costule, between it and the margin, and opening on the inner side next the costule, the sori at length covering almost the whole of the under surface. Veins of the barren pinnules transverse or oblique on the costule, mostly forked. Name from loma, a fringe, in allusion to the scarious in-dusium.

L. Patersoni, Spreng. Rhizome short, thick, ascending. Fronds variable, from a few inches to two feet high, stipes short scaly, entire or pinnatifid with few or several linear segments three to six inches long, more or less decurrent on the rachis and stipes, those of the barren frond half to one inch broad, the veins trans-verse; segments of the fertile fronds as long but only one to two lines broad, the sori at length covering the whole under surface. Like others of this genus the lower portions of the fertile frond, or at times one side, sterile. Common in the dense scrubs of tropical Queensland, also at Maroochie, and again in several loca-lities in Southern Queensland; plentiful also in N. S. Wales, Vic-toria and Tasmania.

L. vulcanica, Blume.   Rhizome thick, or shortly creeping, clothed with shining black hair-like scales.   Fronds under one foot high, glabrous, deeply pinnatifid with numerous segments; those of the barren fronds lanceolate, falcate, confluent by their broad base, the lower ones, one to two inches long, three to six lines broad, the lowest pair scarcely smaller and sometimes reflexed, the upper segments gradually diminished to short lobes. Segments of the fertile fronds nearly as long, under two lines broad except the dilated adnate base.   Tasmania.   The barren fronds collected by N. Taylor on Cape York Peninsula, in Queensland, and by Miss Campbell, in Gippsland, Victoria, being insufficient until fertile fronds are met with to determine.

L. discolor, Willd.   Rhizome caudiciform or trunk-like, erect, sometimes over a foot high.   Fronds numerous, one to two feet long, pinnate or deeply pinnatifid, the rhachis and stipes glabrous and shining black, with scales only at the base of the stipes, lanceolate in outline.   Pinnules of sterile frond one and a half to three inches long, broadly linear or narrow-lanceolate, mostly connected by their dilated base, the lower ones gradually smaller and more distinct, veins not very conspicuous.   Pinnules of the fertile fronds very numerous, one to three inches long, one and half to three lines broad.   This beautiful fern is rare in Queensland, at present only having been met with at Maroochie and Rockingham Bay ; more general in N. S. Wales, Victoria and Tasmania.   In South Australia it is found in gullies of Mount Lofty Ranges.

L. lanceolata, Spreng.   Rhizome also rising into a short trunk. Frond six inches to above one foot long, deeply pinnatifid or pinnate, the rhachis glabrous, of a pale color ; segments of the sterile fronds oblong or lanceolate, dilated at the base, contiguous and often confluent, the longer ones three-quarters to near two inches long and four to six lines broad, the lower one gradually smaller, the lowest very short and broad, texture thinner than in L. discolor. Segment of the fertile fronds about one inch long and one and a half line broad.   Found in Gippsland and a few other parts of Victoria, and many parts of Tasmania, especially in subalpine forest; and at Mount Gambier in South Australia.

L. attenuata, Willd.   Rhizome thick, creeping, densely clothed with long, almost hair-like brown scales.   Fronds one to one and a half feet long, deeply pinnatifid almost pinnate from near the base. Segments of the barren ones lanceolate-falcate, one to two inches long in the centre of the frond, the lower ones gradually smaller, the lowest ones very short and broad, all attached by their broad base and mostly confluent, the rhachis glabrous or slightly scaly.   Veins oblique from the costule, once forked.   Segments of the fertile fronds very narrow linear, two to four inches long.   Australian habitat Lord Howe's Island, where it seems usually found on the stems of tree ferns.

L. alpina, Spreng.   Rhizome creeping scaly.   Fronds deeply pinnatifid or pinnate, three to eight inches long, the rhachis and slender stipes glabrous. Pinnules or segments of the barren fronds oblong, obtuse, attached by their broad base, the larger ones scarcely half-inch long, quarter-inch broad and usually distinct, the upper ones smaller and confluent, the lower gradually smaller, short, broad, and at times distant. Fertile fronds often much longer than the barren ones, the segments two to five lines long, one to one and a half lines broad. Found in the mountainous parts of Victoria and Tasmania and probably N. S. Wales.

L. fluviatilis, Spreng. Rhizome short, thick, scaly. Fronds six inches to over one foot long, pinnate. Pinnæ or segments of barren fronds oblong, rounded at the end, attached by their broad base, the upper ones, half to one inch long, three to four lines broad, all distinct, the rhachis more or less scaly. Segments of fertile fronds six to eight lines long, one to one and a half lines broad. Found in the deep shady valleys of Gippsland, Victoria, and Tasmania.

L. Fullageri, F. v. Muell. Rhizome caudiciform one to two feet high, thickened by the bases of old stipites to three or more inches. Fronds mostly about one foot long, pinnate. Pinnæ of the sterile ones oblong-lanceolate, obtuse, obtusely auriculate at the base on each side, the large ones, one and a half to two inches long, and half an inch broad, the upper ones shorter and confluent, the lower smaller distant and more auriculate, all attached by their broad base, the margins and forked veinlets ciliate, the rhachis densely ferruginous, hispid. Pinnæ of fertile fronds one to two inches long, scarcely one line broad. Only so far as at present known found on Lord Howe's Island, N. S. Wales.

L. capensis, Willd. Pickled Cabbage fern. Rhizome thick, short, and scaly, but in many of the Queensland swamps forming a caudex of several feet in height. Fronds pinnate, the pinnæ of the sterile ones broadly lanceolate, very oblique at the base and attached only by the midrib, the lowest pair not much smaller or very rarely one small pair lower down, otherwise very variable, fronds from one to four feet long, bearing numerous pinnæ from three to six inches long, one inch broad, or the whole frond not over a foot long and much smaller pinnæ. Rhachis scaly or glabrous. Fertile fronds equally variable with the sterile, bearing pinnæ of from one to six inches long, often one half of the frond only fertile. Queensland swamps, north and south, and wet places of all the other colonies and Tasmania.

L. euphlebia, Kunze. Rhizome thick and woody, slightly scaly, ascending to one or more feet. Fronds pinnate, often about two feet long. Pinnæ distant, lanceolate, three to eight inches long, half to three-quarter inch broad, contracted at the base and sometimes tapering to a short petiolule, the uppermost one rarely sessile or slightly decurrent, the lowest not much smaller, the rhachis glabrous. Pinnæ of the fertile fronds narrow-linear, three to six inches long. The only Australian habitat, Rockingham Bay, Queensland.

H

XXVII.—BLECHNUM. LINN.

Rhizome short and thick, or slightly elongated, and horizontal or erect. Fronds pinnate, deeply pinnatifid, or in some species (not Australian) bi-pinnate or even simple. Pinnæ or segments narrow. Sori in a continuous line on each side of the costule, with a membranous indusium opening from under the costule outwards, the two sori often at length confluent, concealing the costule (mid-rib). Name from blechnon, the Greek name of a fern.

B. cartilagineum, Sw. Rhizome short thick, ascending, woody, more or less clothed with shining black scales. Fronds one to two feet long, the stipes usually scabrous. Segments numerous, three to six inches long, almost coriaceous, serrulate. distinctly veined, dilated and adnate at the base, the upper ones smaller and confluent, the lower ones sometimes distinct. Found along creek-sides and borders of scrubs in southern Queensland and N. S. Wales ; also several parts of Gippsland, Victoria.

Var. tropica. Rhizome elongated, ascending or erect, to one foot high, and two or three inches thick, by the persistent bases of old stipites. Frond as in the species, only larger. A very distinct form found on the damp hill-sides Ranges, Rockingham Bay and Trinity Bay. I took this to be identical with Presl's B. nitidum from which Mr. Bentham says (Flora Austr. Vol. VI, 739) it differs.

B. lævigatum, Cav. Rhizome thick and horizontal, very scaly. Fronds one to two feet long. Pinnæ all distinct, obliquely truncate at the base, attached by the costule only, in some fronds all barren, one and half to six inches long, half to one inch broad, entire or serrulate ; in other fronds all fertile, two to five inches long, two lines broad, the sori occupying almost the whole under surface ; in other fronds again four to six inches long, four to six lines broad, with the sori next the costule as in B. cartilagineum, but not adnate to the rhachis. Found so far as known only at Port Jackson and the Blue Mountains in N. S. Wales.

B serrulatum, Rich. Rhizome thick, creeping. Fronds one to four feet long. Pinnæ distinct, linear or lanceolate, mostly two to four inches long and three or four lines broad, obliquely truncate at the base but attached by the mid-rib only serrulate, smooth and shining, the veins oblique, very numerous and fine, mostly forked. Sori close to the mid-rib, indusium soon concealed under them. A fern frequently met with in swamps from Port Jackson to Port Darwin.

B. orientalis, Linn. Rhizome erect, stout at the extremity, and as well as the stipites, covered with scales. Fronds three to six feet long, pinnate. Pinnæ distinct, six inches to near one foot long, half to one inch broad near the base, tapering to a long narrow point, somewhat cuneate at the base, and attached by the mid-rib only, except near the apex of the frond where they are adnate and decurrent on the rhachis, the lower pinnæ are also much abbreviated, margins entire. Veins simple, rarely forked, very close, parallel, horizontal. Sori close to mid-rib, sometimes covering it, indusium firm rigid, of a dark color when old. Adelaide River, North Australia; and Rockingham Bay, Daintree River, Herbert River, and Islands off the coast, Queensland.

XXVIII.—Monogramme. Schkuhr.

Rhizome slender, creeping. Fronds simple, narrow, veinless, except the costa. Sori in a continuous line in the upper part of the frond, in a groove opening along the costa, the margins of the groove forming an indusium along one or both sides of the sorus. Name from the Greek, alluding to the single line of sori.

M. Junghuhnii, Hook. Var. tenella. Rhizome almost filiform, intricately matted, covered with fine hair-like scales. Fronds slender, grass-like, two to six inches high, entire, scarcely half-line broad, flat with a prominent costa in the barren part, the upper fertile half rather broader. Rockingham Bay, Queensland.

XXIX.—Doodia. R. Br.

Rhizome ascending. Fronds pinnate or pinnatifid. Sori oblong or shortly linear, on tranverse veinlets connecting the forked veins proceeding from the mid-rib, in one or two rows parallel to the mid-rib, on each side, with an indusium of the same shape, proceeding from the veinlet and opening on the inner side. Ferns all more or less scabrous. Named in honor of S. Doody, an old author on English Cryptogamic Botany.

D. aspera, R. Br. Prickly fern. Rhizome short, decumbent or ascending black, clothed with shiny black lanceolate scales, which become more dense on the short black bases of the stipites. Fronds erect, rigid, from twelve to over eighteen inches high, the stipes, rhachis and costules muricate or scabrous. Pinnules or segments numerous, all attached by their broad or dilated base, rigidly serrulate, those in the centre of the frond lanceolate-falcate, (in Queensland specimens often over three inches long) about two inches long, the upper ones shorter and more confluent, gradually reduced to the lanceolate point of the frond, (in the Queensland more abruptly ending in a longer segment) the lower segments more distinct, gradually shorter, the lowest reduced to small wing-like appendages to the rhachis. Sori ovate or almost rounded, usually in a single row on each side of the segments at a little distance from the costule, but in the Queensland larger specimens usually in two rows on each side, and the indusium more lunulate and persistent. A common creek-side or scrub fern in Queensland and N. S. Wales, also in several parts of Gippsland, Victoria.

Var. blechnoides, abbreviated pinnæ or segments at base of frond more distant, and sometimes only attached by the midrib. Sori usually smaller and very near the costule in a single row on each side, rarely a few small ones outside the row. So far as known this form is confined to N. S. Wales.

Var. heterophylla. Stipites tufted, slender, fronds one to one and a half feet long, quarter to two inches broad, slightly scabrous, rhachis with a narrow wing, segments very narrow ending in an elongated segment at the apex of from five to six inches long, the abbreviated ones at the base often only forming slight lobes to the wing of rhachis. Fronds not unfrequently forked. Sori close, often confluent, the wing to rhachis also often fertile, sterile fronds rigidly serrulate. Found on rocks at Maroochie.

Var. media. Stipites tufted, scaly, only slightly scabrous. Fronds six to eighteen inches high, half to two inches broad, pinnate in the lower half pinnatifid in the upper ending in an elongated narrow apex of several inches in length; pinnæ and segments remote, linear, obtuse, gradually shorter towards the base and towards the attenuated caudate apex. The common form near Brisbane, Queensland, where it is found on drier land than many other ferns.

Var. caudata. Fronds often decumbent, six to eighteen inches long, rhachis and stipes nearly smooth flexuose, pinnate except near the attenuated, lanceolate apex. Pinnæ membranous, oblong and usually biauriculate one to one and a half inch long, and three or four lines broad in the sterile fronds often narrowed and linear-lanceolate in the fertile fronds, the lower pinnæ often distant. This is the most general form met with in the south of Queensland, N. S. Wales, Victoria and Tasmania, often found on shady damp hill sides and borders of creeks.

XXX.—ASPLENIUM, LINN. SPLEENWORT.

Rhizome creeping, or short and thick, or rising to an arborescent trunk. Sori linear or rarely oblong on veins proceeding from the midrib (costa) or the base of the pinnules or on their branches. Indusium linear or oblong, attached along one side to the vein and opening along the other side. Name from A. privative, and spleen in allusion to some supposed medicinal qualities.

SECTION I. EUASPLENIUM. Sori linear, diverging from the midrib or from the petiole towards the margin, the indusium opening from the upper or inner edge outwards.

A. nidus, Linn. Bird's-nest fern. Rhizome erect, densely rooting. Fronds simple entire, or rarely bifid, lanceolate, sessile or nearly so in large regular tufts hollowed in the centre, two to six feet long, four to eight inches broad, costa shining black. Veins numerous nearly transverse, parallel, simple or forked, connected at the end in an intramarginal line those near the base of the frond often of a dark color. Sori along the upper or inner side of nearly all the veins, near the middle of the frond and upwards, mostly reaching from the costa to half or three-quarters of their length. Found growing on rocks and scrub trees throughout Queensland and many parts of N. S. Wales.

A. simplicifronds, F. v. Muell. Rhizome scaly. Fronds entire one to one half feet long, half to one and a half inch broad, tapering to a point and decurrent on the short stipes, often very numerous forming large tufts on the stems of trees. Veins transverse simple or forked, mostly about one line apart, not connected within the margin. Sori linear, not reaching either the margin or costa. Rockingham Bay, Trinity Bay, Bellenden Ker Ranges and Cape York Peninsula, Queensland.

A. attenuatum, R. Br. Rhizome a short knot or shortly creeping. Fronds linear-lanceolate bordered by distant short teeth, six to eighteen inches long, half to one and a half inch broad, nearly entire for the greater part of their length and tapering into a long point, frequently proliferous at the end, usually broken up in the lower part into a few obovate or oblong laterally adnate segments, the mid-rib scaly-hairy underneath as well as the stipes. Veins very oblique, simple or forked. Sori variable in length, often reaching the mid-rib, rarely the margin. Abundant on damp rocks in southern Queensland, and throughout N. S. Wales.

Var. multilobum, F. v. M. Fronds similar in size, or rather broader, but broken up nearly the whole length into rounded, ovate, serrated segments, the elongated apex proliferous. Found in the Logan district, Queensland: and Richmond River in N. S. Wales.

Var. integrum. Rhizome creeping, a few inches long, slender. Fronds tufted, six to sixteen inches long, half-inch or less broad, oblong, or tapering into an acuminated, proliferous, apex, rounded or decurrent at the base upon the slender hairy stipes. Found on rocks and wet banks at Maroochie, Queensland.

A. Trichomanes, Linn ; European Maiden-hair, spleenwort. A small tufted fern. Fronds two to six inches high, simply pinnate, the rhachis slender, usually black. Pinnæ numerous, obovate, orbicular, or broadly oblong, nearly equal in size, those of the middle of the frond the largest, two to three or rarely four lines long, more or less toothed. Veins forked, radiating from the mid-rib. Sori several on each pinnæ, oblong-linear and distinct when young, uniting in a circular mass when old. Port Jackson and Blue Mountains, in N. S. Wales; many places in Victoria and Tasmania.

A. flabellifolium, Cav. Fan-shaped spleenwort. Rhizome a small knot. Fronds tufted, weak straggling, slender, often proliferous at the apex, six inches to near one and a half feet long, simply pinnate. Pinnæ shortly petiolulate, obliquely obovate, orbicular or fan-shaped, toothed, the larger ones sometimes three-lobed, two to three lines broad in the small Queensland plants, but the more southern forms often over half-inch. Veins few, forked, pinnately diverging from a short mid-rib often divided at the base into three nearly equal branches. Sori several on each pinnæ, linear when young, often confluent when old. On rocks Enoggera Creek, near Brisbane, and Dalrymple Creek, Southern Queensland ; very common in N. S. Wales, Victoria and Tasmania; Mount Lofty Range, Adelaide, South Australia, and also at a few places in Western Australia.

A. paleaceum, R. Br. Rhizome short, tufted. Fronds decumbent or nearly erect, six to over fifteen inches long, simply pinnate, often proliferous at the end, the stipes rhachis and commonly the principal veins hirsute, or densely shaggy with persistent villose patent scales. Pinnæ petiolulate, ovate, ovate lanceolate or fan-shaped, half to over one inch long, irregularly denticulate and sometimes obscurely three-lobed, prominently striate with radiating forked veins more or less joining in a midrib. . Sori linear, often long but not reaching the midrib.   On rocks in the dense scrubs from Rockhampton to Cape York Peninsula.

A. falcatum, Lam.   Rhizome densely clothed with dark brown scales, shortly creeping, usually growing in the masses formed by other epiphytes.   Fronds from one to four feet long, or much longer in many of the Queensland scrubs, pendulous, sub-coriaceous, lanceolate in outline, stipes long, ebeneous, glabrous or sparingly scaly-hirsute, simply pinnate.   Pinnæ shortly petiolulate, oblique, lanceolate, accuminate, serrulate, and usually more or less pinnatifid with short broad dentate lobes and sometimes auriculate at the base, one and a half to four inches long, prominently striate, the veins very . oblique diverging from the base and from the costule.   Sori linear, long, and nearly reaching the margin, or a few quite short. Found on trees throughout Queensland and N. S. Wales. .

A. obtusatum, Forst.   Rhizome thick, scaly.   Fronds four to twelve inches high, the rhachis and stipes usually rather thick, gla-brous or sparingly scaly.   Pinnæ coriaceous, shortly petiolulate, in. the typical form obliquely oblong or ovate-lanceolate, obtuse, three-quarters to one and a half inches long, regularly crenate-toothed, and from that in some varieties to lanceolate, three to five · inches long, toothed or pinnatifid,   Veins from the midrib oblique and forked.   Sori oblong-linear, not reaching the margin, usually several on each side of the midrib oblique equal and parallel. Abundant on maritime rock in Tasmania.

Var. difforme.   Pinnæ obtuse, more or less pinnatifid.   Tas-mania.

Var. lucidum.   Pinnæ obtuse, lanceolate, two to five inches long, obtusely serrulate, with very numerous parallel sori.   Lord Howe's Island, N. S. Wales.

Var. incisum.   Pinnæ lanceolate, three to five inches long, deeply pinnatifid, with a sorus on each lobe.   Lord Howe's Island, N. S. Wales.

A. Hookerianum, Colenso.   Rhizome short.   Fronds about six inches long, slender but rigid, mostly bi-pinnate, the rhachis slightly scaly-hairy.   Primary pinnæ in the lower part of frond half to one inch long, with six to ten distinct oblong-cuneat dentate segments, one to two or rarely three lines long, the lower ones tapering· to a petiolule, the upper ones as well as the upper pinnæ small and con-fluent.   Veins diverging, free.   Sori few, usually only one or two on each segment, large in proportion.   Uncertain if found in N. S. Wales.   Upper Hume River at an. elevation of 4,000 feet, and at the Colac Ranges in Victoria.

A. furcatum, Thunb. Rhizome thick, dark brown, scaly-hairy. Fronds six to eighteen inches high, pinnate or bi-pinnate, slightly scaly-hairy. Pinnæ lanceolate, about one and a half or two inches long, deeply pinnatifid or pinnate ; segments varying from oblong-cuneate, toothed and confluent to linear-lanceolate, distinct and deeply two to four lobed, the segments or lobes all coriaceous, denticulate at the end, striate with few diverging veins. Sori few, large. Grose River, N. S Wales; Grampians, . Darlot's Creek, Victoria ; also King George's Sound, Western Australia.

A. laserpitiifolium, Lam. Rhizome samewhat erect or shortly horizontal, clothed with satiny ferruginous scales at the top. Fronds one to four feet high, stipes dark, glossy, glabrous, three or four times pinnate. Larger primary pinnæ six to twelve inches long, with numerous secondary pinnæ of one to three inches, again pinnate or the upper ones shorter and pinnatifid only, the primary as well as the secondary pinnæ tapering into a pinnatifid point. Ultimate pinnules or segments obovate or oblong-cuneate, toothed, prominently striate with diverging veins, mostly three to. four lines long. Sori several on each segment, linear, usually rather small, often opposite to each other, and opening face to face. Found in the dense scrubs of tropical Queensland growing on rocks, old logs, &c.

SECTION II.—DAREA. Sori oblong or linear, on a vein proceeding from the mid rib in the pinnæ as in Euasplenium, but on a branch parellel to the margin of its teeth or lobes with the indusium opening towards the margin so as to appear marginal.

A. bulbiferum, Forst. Rhizome thick, scaly, erect. Fronds one to two feet long, glabrous or stipes and rhachis scaly, pinnate or bi-pinnate, often proliferous. Primary pinnæ numerous, usually three to four inches long. Pinnules lanceolate, mostly half to one inch long, pinnately toothed, lobed or divided, with a single veinlet to each lobe or tooth ; the whole frond as well as each pinna ending in a lanceolate, toothed or lobed point. Sori large, one to each lobe or tooth, affixed to the central vein, but the rather rigid prominent indusium thrown over towards the margin so as to make the sorus appear marginal. Found in the scrubs of N. S. Wales, Victoria, Tasmania, and at Mount Gambier, South Australia.

A. flaccidum, Forst. Rhizome short and thick, often scaly. Fronds from one to two feet long in Australian form, often much longer in forms of other places, pale green glabrous, pinnate. Pinnæ coriaceous, narrow, three to six inches long, the barren ones toothed, the fertile pinnately divided into linear lobes of two to six lines, each bearing a single rather large sorus attached to the central vein, but the conspicuous indusium thrown over to the upper side so as to appear marginal. Found on rocks, &c., in N. S. Wales, Victoria and Tasmania. .   .

A. pteridioides, Baker. Rhizome short thick. ·Fronds broadly ovate-lanceolate in outline, four to eight inches long, three to five inches broad, glabrous, coriaceous, pinnate. Pinnæ broadly lan-

ceolate, again pinnate or deeply pinnatifid; segments from obovate
to linear-cuneate, a quarter to one inch long, with few obtuse teeth or
short lobes; veins few, branching into the lobes.   Sori linear,
bordering the lobes on a branch of the vein parallel to and very
near the margin ; indusium narrow, proceeding from the nerve and
opening outwards towards the margin.   Lord Howe's Island, N.
S. Wales.

SECTION III.—ATHYRIUM.   Sori small, often curved mostly at
the fork of veins proceeding from the midrib.

A. umbrosum, J. Sm.   Caraway fern.   Rhizome stout ascend-
ing.scaly.   Fronds two to five feet high, one to two feet broad,
bi-tripinnate, stipes clothed with large scales, thick dark at the
base a light green higher and through the many divisions of the
rhachis.   Pinnules membranous, lanceolate or oblong one to two
inches long, deeply pinnatifid or smaller and pinnately toothed ;
veins oblique, usually forked, proceeding from the midrib into the
lobes or teeth, free.   Sori oblong, usually on the vein, below the
fork or partly on one fork and then slightly curved.   Indusium
membranous, proceeding from the vein, and opening on the upper
or inner margin, the sori often at length covering the centre of the
pinnule.   Found in the dense scrubs of Southern Queensland, N.
S. Wales, Victoria and Tasmania.

Var. tenera.   Is a more membranous form having darker and
more slender stipites.   Sori more distant, and the indusium not so
much broken at maturity,.   Sparingly met with near Brisbane ;
plentiful in the Maroochie scrubs.

SECTION IV.—DIPLASIUM.   Sori linear along veins pinnately
diverging from the central vein to each lobe of the pinnule.   Indusium narrow, opening in the same frond, sometimes on one side
sometimes on the other, or on both sides of the vein.

A. Prenticei, Bail.   Proceed. Linn. So. N.S. Wales, IV, 37.
Rhizome an erect caudex of about one foot high, two inches thick,
covered with the black bases of old stipites mixed with black scales.
Fronds one to two feet long, pinnate, stipes and rhachis more or
less covered with black hair-like scales very dense at the base.
Pinnæ petiolate, two to four inches long, linear-lanceolate, serrulate,
or the ends sharply serrate, the base obliquely truncate, terminal
pinnæ five to six inches long, sometimes deeply lobed at the base.
Veins forked, terminating at the margin, the upper veinlet of each
fork except those near the apex, soriferous, sori occupying nearly
the length of veinlets.   Indusium broad firm.   The habit of this
fern is quite that of a Diplazium, but I find no diplazioid sori.
Found in the creeks of the Ranges Trinity Bay, Queensland.

A. japonicum, Thunb.   Rhizome slender creeping.   Fronds
pinnate, one to one and a half feet long, larger pinnæ three to four
inches long, deeply pinnatifid, the lower segments reaching the
shortly scaly hirsute rhachis.   Sori rather short.   Illawarra, N. S.
Wales.   Some doubt exists regarding the Australian habitat of this
Asiatic species.

A. sylvaticum, Presl. Rhizome short, thick and scaly. Fronds pinnate, one to two feet long. Pinnæ membranous, mostly attached by the midrib only, or shortly petiolulate, the larger ones six inches long, three-quarters to one inch broad, regularly pinnatifid, with short rounded denticulate lobes, with a central vein to each lobe and several oblique parallel veinlets proceeding from it, bearing linear sori extending from the midrib almost to the margin; indusia of the section, single or double, upper pinnæ gradually smaller and more entire, the uppermost semi-decurrent or confluent: Rockingham Bay Ranges, Queensland.

A. maximum, Don. Rhizome short and erect or trunk-like and over two feet high. Fronds bipinnate, several feet long and two to three feet broad, the larger pinnæ closely resembling the entire fronds of A. sylvaticum. Secondary pinnæ lanceolate, acuminate, three to six inches long, three-quarter to one inch broad, pinnatifid with short broad denticulate lobes, but the larger ones more deeply so than in A. sylvaticum and the smaller lobes more oblique and acutely toothed, the pinnæ ending in a long lanceolate serrated point, the rhachis glabrous or slightly scaly. Sori narrow linear and indusia entirely those of A. sylvaticum, to which the species is referred by some. Queensland habitat, Rockingham Bay, and Daintree River. In N. S. Wales, Richmond, Macleay and Tweed Rivers.

A. polypodioides, Metten. Trunk erect two to six feet high. Fronds bipinnate, several feet long and two or more feet broad, stipes and rhachis without scales Secondary pinnæ mostly three to four inches long, lanceolate, shortly petiolulate, acuminate, more or less deeply pinnatifid towards the base, the lower lobes lanceolate falcate, minutely serrulate, the upper ones gradually shorter. Sori on the pinnate veins of the lobes as in the preceeding species but much shorter, rather oblong than linear. Indusia of the section opening on one or both sides of the vein. Common in the swamps of Northern Queensland.

A. melanochlamys, Hook. Rhizome erect six inches to one foot high, three to five inches thick. Fronds bipinnate, six feet long, one to two feet broad, widely spreading, darker colored and not so membranous as the last species. Secondary pinnæ deeply pinnatifid,' segments from oblong rounded and under half an inch to lanceolate and above one inch long and then usually crenate with a tooth opposite each sorus. Sori and indusia linear, very conspicuous from their dark almost black color, reaching usually almost from the midrib to the margin. Low land, Lord Howe's Island, N. S. Wales.

A. decussatum, Sw. Trunk erect, scaly. Fronds three to four feet long, pinnate, with a thick smooth rhachis, the stipes somewhat rough and often densely scaly at the base. Pinnæ shortly petiolulate or attached by the midrib only, often proliferous in the axis, lanceolate, acuminate, six inches to near one foot long, one to one and a half inches broad, shortly dentate, the terminal pinna often

I

large, hastato-triangular and pinnatifid. Primary veins proceeding obliquely from the midrib to the teeth or lobes, with secondary obliquely pinnate veinlets often anastomosing. Sori linear, on the secondary veinlets, with single or double indusia. Queensland; Rockingham Bay, and Daintree River.

XXXI.—CYSTOPTERIS, BERNH. BLADDER FERN.

Delicate ferns, with twice or thrice pinnate fronds, with small dentate segments. Veins forked or pinnate, with free venules. Sori small, globular, attached to the concave base of an ovate indusium fixed on a venule at a distance from the margin. Name from two Greek words, of which the English name is a literal translation.

C. fragilis, Bernh. The little bladder fern. Rhizome tufted, scaly. Fronds six to nine inches high, ovate-lanceolate or oblong in their outline, twice pinnate, the longest primary pinnæ one to one and a half inches long, decreasing towards the ends, on a slender stipes without scales. Segments ovate or lanceolate, pinnatifid or dentate, with obtuse lobes or teeth. Sori several on each segment, at first enclosed in the indusium which is small and thin in the Australian form and soon disappears under the enlarged globular sori. On the wet rocks of Mount Olympus, and Lake St. Clair, Tasmania.

XXXII.—ASPIDIUM, SW. SHIELD FERN.

Rhizome thick and shortly erect, or creeping. Fronds twice or thrice pinnate or even more, while in some species (not Australian) the fronds are simple. Indusium orbicular, covering the sorus when young, attached by the centre or by a point or in a sinus on one side, so that when opened all round by the growth of the spore-cases it becomes peltate or more or less reniform. Name from aspis, a shield, from the form of indusium.

A. cordifolium, Sw. Rhizome emitting wiry rooting fibres, which often bear fleshy tubers the size of a pigeon's egg, all beautifully clothed with linear-lanceolate transparent netted scales. Fronds pendulous from one to two or more feet long, simply pinnate. Pinnæ very numerous, often overlapping one another, approximate, sessile or nearly so, and articulate on the very scaly rhachis, oblong, rounded and usually denticulate at the end, about one inch long, obliquely cordate at the base, with the upper auricle much the largest, gradually smaller at the end of the frond, and the lowest pinnæ short, broad and barren. Veins obliquely diverging from the costule or midrib of pinna, forked or branched. Sori terminating each upper branch, forming a row at some distance from the margin. Indusium reniform, very prominent, attached in a deep sinus. Found in many parts of Queensland, either growing among rocks or in the masses formed by epiphytes upon scrub trees; very abundant upon the Glasshouse Mountains; also at Clarence and Richmond Rivers, and Lord Howe's Island, in N. S. Wales.

A. exaltatum, Sw. Rhizome similar to the last but stronger and not forming tubers. Fronds erect, strong, two to five feet long, simply pinnate, the rhachis usually covered with a dense scaly tomentum. Pinnæ numerous, nearly sessile, articulate on the rhachis, lanceolate, mostly acuminate and crenate, obliquely truncate at the base and at times auriculate on the upper side; the longest ones three to six inches long, with numerous fine forked veins obliquely diverging from the midrib, the lower pinnæ usually shorter, rounded at the end and barren. Sori terminating one branch of the veins, forming a regular row usually close to the margin. Indusium almost orbicular, laterally attached in a deep sinus, or sometimes peltate and opening all round. Very common on the coast rocks of tropical Queensland.

Var. longipinna. Pinnæ often six inches long and three-quarter inch broad, with the sori at a greater distance from the margin. This form is given in the Flora Austr., but the size and form of the pinnæ differ so considerable in the species as to make it almost impossible to mark distinct forms; at times the pinnæ is of a very firm coriaceous texture with a glossy surface, and the sori mid-way between margin and midrib.

A. ramosum, Beauv. Rhizome slender, scaly, creeping up trees, over rocks, &c., often to a great length. Fronds varying from a few inches to over one foot long, pinnate. Pinnæ numerous, obliquely oblong, obtuse, crenate, very oblique at the base, articulate on the rhachis, the lower side narrowed, the upper broadly truncate and often auriculate, one to two inches long, and three to four lines broad, but at times much smaller. Veins diverging from the midrib, once or twice forked. Sori in a regular row between the midrib and margin. Indusium orbicular, usually attached in a deep sinus, but sometimes peltate. The fronds of this variable species are sometimes thickly clothed with hairs. A very abundant fern in tropical Queensland scrubs, also in a few places in Southern Queensland, and in many parts of N. S. Wales.

A. unitum, Sw. Rhizome creeping. Fronds one to two feet long on long stipites, simply pinnate, pubescent or glabrous. Pinnæ narrow-lanceolate, three to six inches long, sessile but not adnate, or the lower ones on short petiolules, firm, regularly pinnatifid, the lobes usually reaching to about the middle, broad, rounded or acute, often falcate. Veins pinnate to each lobe, the veinlets of adjoining lobes uniting in a vein leading to the sinus. Sori at the end of the veinlets forming usually a close row along the margin of the lobes. Indusium orbicular-reniform or almost peltate, very small and soon disappearing. N. Australia; near most swamps in Queensland. Common also in N. S. Wales; also in Western Australia.

A. pteroides, Sw. Rhizome creeping. Fronds one to three feet high, pinnate usually more membranous than A. unitum, but in form somewhat like that species, glabrous or minutely pubescent, stipes long and sometimes scaly at the base. Pinnæ four to eight inches long and about half an inch broad, often petiolulate, the lower scarcely˙ smaller, lobes reaching three-quarter way to midrib or nearly so. Sori rather large quite marginal and confined to the lobes not reaching below the sinuses. Indusium orbicular-reniform. Rockingham and Trinity Bays, Queensland.

A. molle, Sw. Rhizome short thick, one to two feet high on stipites of equal length, simply pinnate, nearly glabrous or quite hairy, of a light soft green color. Pinnæ lanceolate, the longer ones three to six inches long, or more often acuminate, regularly pinnatifid, the lobes sometimes short, sometimes reaching above half-way to the midrib, the pinnæ truncate at the base, mostly sessile, the lower ones gradually smaller and more distant. Veins pinnate in each lobe and prominent, the branches or veinlets of adjoining lobes united in a vein tending to the sinus. Sori usually in a row about half way between the midrib of the lobe and the margin. Indusium orbicular-reniform, often disappearing early. Common throughout Queensland and N. S. Wales in various situations.

Var. didymosorus. Sori one or two to each lobe and only at the junction of the lowest veinlets of adjoining lobes. Rockingham Bay, Queensland.

Var. truncatum. This seems only to differ from the typical form in size, on the Tweed River; it is said to attain the height of seven to eight feet, with pinnæ eight inches or more long the lobes at times truncate. Duck Creek, Richmond and Tweed Rivers, N. S. Wales.

A. confluens, Metten. Rhizome thick, scaly, erect. Fronds one to three feet long, deeply pinnatifid, pinnate usually at the base, or the frond somewhat tripartite. Stipes very dark. Segments lanceolate, often numerous, the upper ones two to six inches long, pinnately toothed or lobed, confluent on a broadly winged rhachis, the intermediate ones six to ten inches long, deeply pinnatifid and decurrent on the rhachis, the lowest pair quite free at the base, pinnatifid with long lanceolate lobes, of which the outer ones are again pinnatifid, all membranous. Veins copiously netted. Sori scattered, either on short veinlets free in the areoles or on the anastomosing veinlets. Indusium when perfect rather large, orbicular, peltate or on the same frond attached by a deep sinus. Found in most of the scrubs of tropical Queensland.

A aculeatum, Sw. Lady fern. Rhizome short and thick, suberect. Fronds one to two feet high, twice pinnate, sometimes proliferous, the lower part of the stipes and the whole frond when young very shaggy with dark brown scarious scales mixed with hair-like ones. Primary pinnæ lanceolate in outline, one and a half to four inches long, the lower ones decreasing in length; pinnules ovate-lanceolate, curved, three to six lines long, prickly-toothed, with a prominent angle or lobe on the upper or inner side. Veins forked, diverging from the costule. Sori usually six to eight on each pinnule. Met with in Southern Queensland; many places in N. S. Wales; from Portland and the Grampians to Gippsland in Victoria; and abundant in Tasmania.

A. aristatum, Sw. Rhizome long, creeping, crinite with long subulate ferruginous scales. Fronds one to two feet high, broadly ovate-triangular in outline, twice pinnate on the lower pinnæ, again pinnate at the base, thin, firm, of a light glossy green color, the stipes scaly-hairy at the base. Pinnules or lobes very obliquely oblong or lanceolate, half to one inch long, narrowed or cuneate at the base, bordered at the end by a few teeth ending in bristle-like points. Veins forked, diverging from the costule. Sori small, not numerous, loosely arranged in two rows. Indusium small, orbicular-reniform. Enoggera, near Brisbane; Port Denison and Rockingham Bay, in Queensland; New England, Hastings and Tweed Rivers, and Illawarra, in N. S. Wales.

A. capense, Willd. Rhizome creeping. Fronds from under one foot to two feet high, broad, rigid, the stipes and rhachis scaly, mostly bipinnate but the smaller ones occasionally simply pinnate. Pinnæ coriaceous, lanceolate, toothed or pinnatifid, with reticulate veins concealed in the thick tissue. Sori often large, one to each tooth or lobe. Indusium peltate and rigid, fallen mostly from old sori. A common fern in N. S. Wales, Victoria and Tasmania.

Var. Moorei. Lord Howe's Island. Fronds two to three feet long, rhachis very shaggy with large light brown scales.

A. decompositum, Spreng. Rhizome shortly creeping. Fronds glabrous or the rhachis and primary nerves pubescent or scaly; very variable in size and outline, usually from one to two feet high, the stipes often long, pinnate with deeply pinnatifid pinnæ, the larger ones thrice pinnate. Primary and secondary pinnæ ending in a narrow pinnatifid apex. Pinnules or segments lanceolate, two to three lines broad, pinnately toothed or lobed, the teeth acute or mucronate and the margin of the lobes usually nerve-like. Veins pinnate more or less divided according to the divisions of the pinnules. Sori usually one or two to each principal lobe not very far from the costule. Indusium orbicular-reniform often concealed as the sorus enlarges and sometimes perhaps deficient from the first. Very common in Queensland, N. S. Wales, Victoria and Tasmania, also at Penola in S. Australia.

A. acuminatum, T. Moore. Rhizome shortly creeping. Fronds ovate-lanceolate, in outline bipinnate, in the lower parts six to twelve inches long, on slender stipites, which are nearly glabrous, while the rhachis and costules are usually hispid. Veins pinnate ending in marginal teeth. Pinnules oblong, obtuse, but the end of frond and lower pinnæ elongated and either lobed or toothed. Sori near the midrib. Indusium large somewhat firm in texture, orbicular-reniform. My only specimens of this beautiful and distinct fern are from near Sale, Gippsland, Victoria, but it is likely to be met with in many other parts of Southern Australia.

A. tenerum, Spreng. Rhizome shortly creeping, thick, often a good deal branched. Fronds somewhat coriaceous glabrous and glossy above, but the stipes, rhachis, and costules hairy, with a few scattered dark brown scales, bi-tripinnate in general outline resem-

bling A. decompositum. Segments obtusely or acutely toothed or
lobed very regular. Veins pinnate, venules free. Sori close to the
margin round which it usually forms a line. Indusium orbicular-
reniform, large, or quite small on fronds from the same rhizome.
Found in many Queensland scrubs from Brisbane to Rockhampton;
also at the Richmond, Bellinger and Tweed Rivers in N. S.
Wales.

Var. apicale. Lord Howe's Island, N. S. Wales. This form
differs but little from the typical plant.

A. tenericaule, Thw. Rhizome short and thick or creeping.
Fronds one to three feet long on a stipes of one to two feet, twice
pinnate, the larger primary pinnæ six to eight inches long. Pinnules lanceolate, one to one and a half inch long on the larger
pinnæ, very deeply pinnatifid with numerous lanceolate lobes one to
three lines long, all more or less decurrent, ciliate on the margins as
well as the principal veins and rhachis with rigid white hairs or
bristles. Veins branched in each lobe but free. Sori one to six in
each lobe, small and distinct with few spore-cases, or larger and confluent. Indusium very small and only to be seen on young sori.
Queensland, Rockingham Bay, Bowen, and Daintree River. N.
S. Wales, Clarence River. The Flora Australiensis speaks of the
above fern having been found at these places, but probably there is
some mistake, for the form found near Brisbane, and which has been
taken for it, is a true Polypodium and as such will be found in this
work as P. pallidum.

A. hispidum, Sw. Rhizome thick, creeping, covered with brown
scales. Fronds one to two feet long, broadly ovate or triangular in
outline, usually tripinnate with acuminate pinnæ, the stipes stout
and with the primary and secondary rhachis hispid with long fine
spreading dark colored hairs or bristles. Pinnules lanceolate deeply
pinnatifid, quarter to half an inch long, deeply and sharply toothed.
Veins solitary on each lobe or tooth. Sori solitary on the smaller
segments or lobes. Indusium orbicular, attached by a lateral sinus
or almost peltate. Found on the Cape Otway Ranges, Victoria.

B. No indusium.

XXXIII.—POLYPODIUM, LINN.

Rhizome creeping in nearly all the Australian species with small
brown scales with a broad adnate base and more or less acute or
subulate points. Fronds simple pinnate or compound. Sori
orbicular very rarely oblong, variously dispersed over the under
surface, without indusium. Name derived from the Greek and
literally means many footed, and said to be given on account of the
early stages of growth being supposed to be similar in appearance
to the feelers of a Polypus.

SERIES I. DIANEURA.—Veins pinnate, the venules diverging
from a midrib, simple or forked, the branches free. Sori inserted
on a simple branch or fork, the other fork often again forked.

P. australe, Metten. Rhizome short, sub-erect, scaly. Fronds entire, coriaceous, linear or oblanceolate, various as to size from one to six inches long, contracted into a short stipes. Veins diverging from the costa, one or more forked, free, but concealed by the thick texture of the frond. Sori oblong or linear, oblique and parallel in a single row on each side of the costa, when old often confluent and covering nearly the whole surface. Mount Lindsay and Maroochie in Queensland; abundant on trees and rocks in N. S. Wales, Victoria and Tasmania.

P. Hookeri, Brackenr. Rhizome short, ascending. Fronds usually two to four inches but said at times to reach eight inches long, coriaceous entire linear or lanceolate, tapering into a very short stipes and always fringed and sprinkled with long spreading dark colored hairs. Veins simple or rather more divided than in the last. Sori orbicular, oval or shortly oblong, rather large, in a single row on each side of the costa. Found on the wet rocks of Trinity Bay, Rockingham Bay Ranges, Queensland; and Lord Howe's Island, in N. S. Wales.

P. blechnoides, Hook. Rhizome stout, clothed with dense linear scales. Fronds two to four inches long, coriaceous, deeply pinnatifid. Segments lanceolate almost reaching to the rhachis, but dilated and shortly confluent at the base, the larger ones in the middle of the frond three to five lines long, the lower ones shorter and broader, contracted into a short narrowly winged stipes. Veins pinnate in each lobe. Sori at the end of the veinlets, orbicular, three to five pairs in each lobe, forming two rows nearer to the margin then to the midrib. Queensland, Rockingham Bay.

P. grammitidis, R. Br. Rhizome short, scaly. Fronds four to eight inches long (much longer in New Zealand), coriaceous, once or twice pinnatifid. Primary segments linear or narrow-lanceolate, reaching almost to the rhachis but more or less decurrent and confluent, the longer ones in the middle of the frond one to one and a half inch long, pinnatifid with the lobes mostly very short and obtuse, but occasionally some of them linear and three to four lines long, the lower primary segments often shortly linear and entire, the lowest decurrent on the stipes, rarely almost all the segments linear and entire. Veins pinnate in the linear segments, almost simple in the short lobes. Sori orbicular or oval, varying from one to four according to the length of the lobe. Victoria; Fern-tree Gullies, Dandenong Ranges; abundant also in Tasmania, often forming matted patches on damp rocks.

P. tenellum, Forst. Rhizome long, creeping over rocks and up the stems of scrub trees to a good height by means of adventitious roots like ivy, the young part clothed with scales. Fronds distant or clustered six to twenty-four inches long, glabrous, simply pinnate, the stipes articulated to the rhizome. Pinnæ shortly petiolulate and articulate on the rhachis, lanceolate, acuminate, often falcate, undulate-crenate, unequal at the base, two to four inches long, membranous. Veins pinnate with forked branches, one fork bearing the sorus, the other again forked. Sori orbicular, small or large, sometimes not very close, forming a row very near the margin. A common climbing fern of the South Queensland scrubs, also in some of the northern scrubs; common throughout N. S. Wales.

P. punctatum, Thunb. Rhizome long, slender, creeping, densely scaly. Fronds one to four feet high, much branched, stipes often long slender usually of a dark brown color, bi-tripinnate. Pinnules oblong, half to one and a half inch long, membranous or rather rigid when in full fruit, deeply pinnatifid with dentate segments. Veins in each pinnule or segment pinnate with free forked branches. Sori orbicular in two rows on the smaller pinnules or longer lobes. A very common fern on the borders of Queensland scrubs where, supported by surrounding shrubs, it often attains the height of seven to eight feet. From its great similarity to Hypolepis tenuifolia it is often mistook for that species both being glandular pubescent. If in fruit the position of the sori in P. punctatum will be at a distance from the margin, while that of H. tenuifolia will be marginal. If the plants are sterile the Polypodium will be usually of a more wiry growth.

P. pallidum, Brack. Rhizome short, horizontal, thick, clothed with bright glossy pale colored scales. Fronds one to four feet high. Stipes stout at the base and clothed with soft hair-like scales which soon fall, leaving the stipes glabrous and pale or glaucous, as well as the rhachis, bi-tripinnate, the larger pinnæ one foot or more long, secondary pinnæ lanceolate two to four inches long, pinnules linear obtuse half to one and a half inch long and more or less connected by the narrow wing of the costa, the whole plant more or less covered with white glandular hairs. Veins pinnate. Sori from a few to fourteen on a lobe; when ripe the spore-cases often of a dark color, all small and usually but a few in each sorus. Found at Enoggera Creek, near Brisbane. There is not the least doubt but that this fern is a true Polypodium, but in the Flora Australiensis it seems placed with Aspidium tenericaule, Thw, a mistake likely to occur from the examination of dried specimens, but never from living ones. The name used is appropriate, and the plant is most likely identical with that of Brackenridge, but none of his authentic specimens are in the colony, so there is some doubt on this point.

P. aspidioides, Bail. Shiny fern. Rhizome horizontal, thin, shortly creeping. Fronds twelve to eighteen inches long, usually ovate-lanceolate in the small forms, but more triangular-ovate in the larger, in outline; the stipes long, slender, sulcate and densely covered at or near the base with dark brown ovate acuminate scales, bi-tripinnate; the pinnæ and pinnules much elongated at the apex, the upper surface glossy, rhachis and costules hairy. Veins pinnate, ending beyond the margin in aculeate teeth. Sori medial. Found abundant in the Brisbane River scrubs, where it may at once be detected by the shining upper surface of its fronds. This beautiful fern has been for a long time confused with Lastrea acuminata, T. Moore, the Aspidium acuminatum, Hort. Ang., and from which it only differs in the entire absence of indusium and in the longer more aculeate marginal teeth.

Var. tropica. This fern has been thought to be identical with the species called by Blume P. rufescens. It differs slightly from P. aspidioides in wanting the gloss on the upper surface of frond and being less divided, also the marginal teeth are at times wanting and the obtuse pinnule only crenulated, a soft pubescence with a reddish tinge covers the whole frond; all these variations might be due to climate, the form only being met with in the tropics. Ranges Trinity Bay, Queensland.

SERIES II.—SYNNEURA. Veins pinnate under each lobe of the pinnæ, the branches simple, uniting with corresponding branches of the vein of the adjoining lobe. Sori usually placed towards the end of the upper branches of the series.

P. proliferum, Presl. Rhizome shortly creeping. Fronds weak, one to two or more feet long, proliferous at the apices and axils of the pinnæ, thus widely extending, pinnate. Pinnæ lanceolate, one to four inches long, often interrupted by the formation of the axillary plants, shortly and regularly pinnatifid with obtuse rounded lobes, sometimes almost reduced to crenatures, broadly truncate at the base. Veins pinnate to each lobe, the branches or veinlets of adjoining lobes uniting in a vein leading to the sinus. Sori in two rows to each lobe, sometimes only at the end, sometimes reaching almost to the midrib of pinnæ. Albert River, North Australia; very abundant in tropical Queensland, on the edge of rivers and swamps; also in a few places in Southern Queensland, and the Clarence River, N. S. Wales.

P. urophyllum, Wall. Rhizome creeping, often several inches below the surface. Fronds two to four feet long on a stipes often nearly as long, pinnate, more or less glandular-pubescent underneath. Pinnæ six inches to nearly one foot long, one to two inches broad, acuminate, regularly and broadly crenate or shortly lobed, rounded or truncate at the base. Primary veins leading to the lobes numerous and parallel, pinnate, the branches or veinlets uniting in an intermediate vein leading to the sinus. Sori orbicular in two regular rows between each primary veins, extending from the midrib of the pinnæ to the margin. Ranges about Rockingham Bay, Daintree River, and Cape York Peninsula. In venation this species resembles Meniscium cuspidatum, Blume.

P. Hillii, Baker. Rhizome creeping. Fronds one and a half feet high, pinnate, densely and softly hirsute all over. Pinnæ about nine, the three terminal ones small, the others oblong, four to six inches long, one and a half to two inches broad, pinnately crenate or shortly lobed, but not so regularly so as in P. urophyllum. Parallel primary pinnate veins leading to the lobes, the branches or venules uniting in an intermediate vein reaching the sinus. Sori as in P. urophyllum, in two rows between each two primary veins, reaching from the midrib to the margin, but not close. Very little is known of this fern, it having only once been met with, few

K

specimens preserved, and the plant not in cultivation at the present time. Habitat somewhere between Cape Cleveland and Rockingham Bays.

P. pœcilophlebium, Hook. Rhizome creeping. Fronds six inches to one foot long on a stipes of about the same length, pinnate, glabrous, dark green. Pinnæ lanceolate, acuminate, four to eight inches long, one to one and a half inches broad, shortly contracted into a petiolule. Primary parallel veins numerous and prominent, pinnate, the branches or veinlets oblique, more or less anastomosing with those of the adjoining primary vein, but not forming a straight intermediate vein as in the other species of this series. Sori rather small, in two irregular rows between each two primary veins. Very common in the scrubs of tropical Queensland.

SERIES III.—DICTYOPHLEBIA. Venation reticulate. Primary veins proceeding from the midrib more or less distinctly parallel, connected by transverse anastomosing veinlets, enclosing areoles, in some of which are short free, usually clavate, veinlets. Sori placed either on the free veinlets or on the connecting branches.

P. serpens, Forst. Rhizome slender, creeping, often forming large matted patches on trees and rocks. Fronds small, entire, coriaceous, obtuse, contracted into a short stipes, densely covered with stellate scales, the barren ones obovate or oblong, from under half to two and a half inches long, the fertile ones linear or oblong-linear, three-quarters to two inches long. Venation reticulate, concealed in the thick texture of the frond, the dry fronds rugose with indented lines not connected with the veins. Sori irregularly crowded in the upper part of the frond and often confluent. Abundant in Queensland, N. S. Wales and Victoria.

P. confluens, R. Br. Rhizome creeping to a great extent over rocks, tree trunks, &c. Fronds entire, coriaceous, obtuse, or rarely somewhat acuminate, contracted into the stipes, covered with stellate scales, which are often deciduous on the old fronds, varying much in length, both in sterile and fertile fronds from one inch to one foot, but always narrow and thick. Veins reticulate, but concealed in the texture of frond. Sori large, oval or oblong in a row on each side of the costa and often confluent. A very abundant fern throughout Queensland and N. S. Wales.

P. acrostichoides. Forst. Rhizome creeping, wiry, often forming large masses on coast trees. Fronds lanceolate, entire or forked, six inches to two feet long, contracted into a short stipes, coriaceous and thick concealing the venation which is reticulate, under surface clothed with stellate scales, upper nearly glabrous. Sori in the upper portion of the frond small, distinct, very numerous in several rows between the margin and the costa. Along the tropical coast of Queensland.

P. attenuatum, R. Br. Rhizome shortly creeping. Fronds entire, coriaceous, linear-lanceolate, obtuse or shortly acuminate, six to eighteen inches long, quarter to half an inch broad, contracted into a short stipes, glabrous, the reticulate venation concealed in the thick texture. Sori large, oval-oblong, inserted in a single row on each side of costa half-way between it and the margin. Rather plentiful on rocks in the ranges of Queensland, both North and South ; and also throughout N. S. Wales.

P. simplicissimum, F. v. M. Rhizome creeping. Fronds lanceolate, acuminate, entire or slightly crenate, four to ten inches long, tapering into a short stipes, rather thin, glabrous, prominently penniveined with intermediate reticulations and free veinlets in the areoles. Sori rather large, orbicular, in a single row on each side of the costa half-way between it and the margin, the receptacle scarcely excavated and obscurely or not at all prominent on the upper surface. Rockingham Bay, Queensland.

P. nigrescens, Blume. Rhizome creeping. Fronds two to three feet high on a stipes of one foot, or more, glabrous, deeply pinnatifid. Segments lanceolate, acuminate with a narrow point, membranous, six inches to one foot long, one to one and a half inch broad, confluent at the base in a broad wing to the costa ; the main veins very distinct, reticulate between them, with numerous free veinlets in the areoles. Sori large in the centre of the large areoles, distant in a single row on each side of the costule at a distance from it, the receptacle deeply excavated and very prominent on the upper surface. Daintree River, Queensland.

P. phymatodes, Linn. Rhizome creeping. Fronds two to three or more feet high, deeply pinnatifid, smooth and glabrous. Segments lanceolate, four to eight inches long, three-quarter to one and a half inch broad, confluent at the base into a broadly winged costa, the costule of each lobe very prominent, with copious reticulations between the primary veins, but all concealed in the smooth though not thick texture of the frond. Sori rather large, orbicular or oval, distant in about two rows or rarely in a single row on each side of the costule at some distance from it, the receptacles slightly excavated and prominent on the upper surface. There is little or nothing to separate the Australian form of P. nigrescens, Bl., from this species. Common near the coast of tropical Queensland.

P. pustulatum, Forst. Rhizome stout, creeping. Fronds entire or deeply pinnatifid, three-quarter to one and a half feet high, with few segments. Segments oblong-lanceolate, mostly acuminate, three to six inches long, four to eight lines broad, confluent at the base into a broad-winged costa, of a firm membranous texture showing on the under side the primary veins, with copious intermediate reticulations, and free veinlets in the areoles. Sori orbicular, rather large, distant in a single row on each side of the costa at a distance from it and often near the margin. Receptacles excavated, more or less prominent on the upper surface. N. S. Wales, Victoria and Tasmania, rather plentiful, creeping over rocks, trunks of trees, &c. A much smaller plant but very closely allied to the last.

P. scandens, Forst. Rhizome slender, creeping over rocks and

up the trunks of trees, often to a great height. Fronds most
various in outline, six inches to one and a half feet long, entire or
deeply pinnatifid, membranous, segments on pinnatifid frond often
numerous, narrow lanceolate or linear and often falcate, decurrent
and confluent to the wing of costa.   Veins slightly prominent,
forming one or two series of rather large oblong areoles, including
free veinlets.   Sori distant, in a single row on each side of costa
or costules, sub-marginal, the excavated receptacles prominent on
the upper surface.   Enoggera Creek, Maroochie, &c., Queensland;
more frequent in N. S. Wales and Victoria.

P. verrucosum, Wall.   Rhizome creeping.   Fronds three to
four feet long, pinnate, glabrous.   Pinnæ oblong-lanceolate,
acuminate, obtusely serrulate, equally or unequally cuneate at the
base, shortly petiolulate or almost sessile, apparently articulate on
the rhachis, six to eight inches long, half to one inch broad,
membranous. Venation reticulate between the primary veins, with
free venules in the areoles.   Sori distant in a single row on each
side of the costule and near to it, the excavated receptacles very
prominent on the upper surface.   Rockingham Bay and Daintree
River, Queensland; rare.

P. subauriculatum, Blume.   Rhizome horizontal.   Fronds one
to three or sometimes more feet long, glabrous, pinnate.   Pinnæ
linear-lanceolate, mostly acuminate, entire or serrulate, three to six
inches long, three to five lines broad, truncate, rounded or auriculate
at the base, nearly sessile but somewhat articulate on the rhachis.
Venation reticulate between the primary veins, with free veinlets in
the areoles.   Sori distant in a single row on each side of the costule
and near it, the excavated receptacles usually prominent on the
upper surface.   On rocks and trees, scrubs, Northern Queensland.

P. rigidulum, Swartz.   Rhizome short, thick, creeping, usually
on rocks or trees.   Fronds very various, pinnate, scarcely lobed, or
deeply pinnatifid, the pinnate form bearing the sori which is never
found on the sessile, lobed or pinnatifid fronds, rhachis always
pubescent or densely woolly when young.   Pinnæ narrow-lanceolate,
usually rigid and very prominently and copiously reticulate, three
to nine inches long, three to nine lines broad, obliquely or equally
cuneate at the base, often shortly petiolulate, articulate on the
rhachis.   Sori orbicular, distant in a single row on each side of the
costule and not far from it, the excavated receptacles prominent on
the upper surface.   Each of the tall pinnate fronds closely
supported by a broad sessile, usually shortly lobed, almost scarious,
one of about six to twelve inches long, and three or four inches
wide; these fronds are sometimes double this size and then deeply
pinnatifid, very prominently reticulate.   A fern most frequently
met with on rocks throughout Queensland ; also on the Blue
Mountains, N. S. Wales.

Var. Vidgeni.   There are no fronds with articulate pinnæ in
this form, their place is taken by a higher developed state of the
greater number, of the usually sessile scarious fronds peculiar to P.

quercifolium and P. rigidulum. Fronds two to three feet high,
pinnate. Pinnæ on rather long somewhat flattened petiolules, the
margin much incised, cuneate at the base, not articulate upon the
rhachis, more membranous than in the typical form and although
having the same tomentum on the early growth this is soon lost
and the whole plant assumes a beautiful glossy green ; no sori has
been noticed on any of the fronds of this form, but should it be
produced on these nonarticulate fronds then P. rigidulum will fall to
a form of P. quercifolium. Found in a small scrub at Oxley,
Brisbane River, by J. G. Vidgen, Esq., Hon. Sec. Queensland
Acclimatisation Society, in 1875. As a scenic plant this will be
found eminently useful.

P. quercifolium, Linn. Rhizome broad, creeping. Fronds of
two kinds, the small sessile ones similar to the last species, the
large ones two to three feet high, deeply pinnatifid ; segments
lanceolate, six to nine inches long, three-quarter to one and a half
inch broad, decurrent on the rhachis and usually confluent into a
broad wing but sometimes interrupted between the lower segments,
thin but usually rigid, very prominently and copiously reticulated,
the free veinlets within the areoles small and rare. Sori small,
scattered, few or numerous. Usually a coast fern, found from
Rockhampton to Cape York; also in N. Australia.

P. irioides, Poir. Rhizome stout, shortly creeping. Fronds
entire or lobed, one to three feet long, one to three inches broad,
coriaceous, contracted into a short stipes. Primary parallel veins
distant and usually conspicuous with copious fine reticulations
between them, the free veinlets in the areoles numerous. Sori often
small and very numerous, covering the whole under surface of the
upper part of the frond but quite distinct from each other. Found
along the coast from Moreton Bay to Cape York, lining the edge
of rivers and swamps.

XXXIV.—Notholæna, R. Brown.

Rhizome tufted. Fronds usually small, once, twice or three
times pinnate with small lobed segments. Veinlets forked from a
central nerve or from the base of the segment. Sori small at the
ends of the veinlets, almost contiguous forming an apparently
continuous line within the unaltered margin, which is, however, more
or less curved over them in a young state. With regard to the
Australian species it might have been well for them to have been
placed in Cheilanthes. Name derived from the Greek nothos,
spurious; and chlaina, a covering. This latter word is contracted in
several other botanical names to Læna, in the present it alludes to
the edge of the frond curving over the sori and forming a spurious
indusium.

N. pumilio, R. Br. Rhizome short. Fronds tufted, one to
three inches high, simply pinnate, with a filiform rhachis. Pinnæ
few, ovate or oblong, obtuse, three to five lines long, membranous,

without scales, entire on the lower ones with a short lateral lobe on one or both sides, the upper ones confluent. Veins obliquely diverging from the midrib. Sori continuous round the margin except at the base, the margin of the frond at first turned over them, but afterwards flat and not altered in consistence. N. Australia, Port Darwin; Queensland, Endeavour River.

N. vellea, R. Br. Rhizome short. Fronds tufted, mostly about six inches high but sometimes double that height, oblong-lanceolate in outline, pinnate or bipinnate, with a hairy rhachis. Pinnæ half to one inch long, deeply pinnatifid or pinnate, somewhat thick, green and hispid above, very densely woolly hirsute and often ferruginous underneath, the lobes or segments ovate or rounded, very obtuse. Sori at the end of the forked veins forming an almost continuous narrow line round the margin. Port Darwin and several other places in N. Australia; many localities in Northern Queensland; a few places in the interior of N. S. Wales and South Australia; also Fraser's Range, in Western Australia.

N. distans, R. Br. Rhizome short, erect, forming a close knot. Fronds three to six inches high, about an inch broad, ferruginous hirsute above, paleaceous beneath with lanceolate scales, pinnate or bipinnate, primary pinnæ petiolulate often opposite or nearly so, erect-patent, the lowest pair often distant, pinnules obtuse, margins recurved. Sori continuous along the margin. Common in all the Australian Colonies, usually met with on rocks in more exposed situations than most ferns. The species scarcely differs from N. vellea to which it had better perhaps been added as a form.

N. fragilis, Hook. Rhizome horizontal, rather thick, scaly. Fronds broadly deltoid in outline, in some specimens one to one and a half inch long, on slender stipes twice as long, in others three inches long and broad, with firmer black stipes twice or thrice as long, pinnate with numerous small deeply pinnatifid pinnules, the ultimate lobes under one line long, each one bearing a sorus large in proportion, partial rhachis and under side of the lobes hispid with a few rigid hairs or bristles. North Australia, Fitzmaurice River and Port Darwin.

XXXV.—GRAMMITIS, SWARTZ.

Rhizome short, tufted, or sometimes creeping to a great length. Fronds pinnate pinnatifid or entire. Veins forked free or reticulate Sori linear or oblong, on veins diverging from the midrib, scattered or crowded usually in lines, like writing, whence the name, from gramme, writing.

G. Reynoldsii, F. v. M. Rhizome creeping. Fronds in the few specimens seen three to six inches long, simply pinnate. Pinnæ in distant pairs, broadly ovate or orbicular, obtuse, entire, about half an inch long, thick and densely covered on both sides with hair-like scales. Sori buried under the scales, oblong or shortly linear, transverse and distinct but closely crowded near the margin forming a continuous line about one line broad. Found near Mount Olgar, Central Australia.

G. Muelleri, Hook. Rhizome scaly, shortly creeping. Fronds six to twelve inches long, simply pinnate, the rhachis sealy. Pinnæ in distant pairs, ovate or oblong, obtuse, entire, half to one inch long, thick, sprinkled above and densely covered underneath with eiliate seales. The early fronds simple eordate. Sori nearly buried under the seales, very numerous, mostly short, transverse but crowded in an apparently continuous line round the margin, usually about a line and a half broad. Queensland, Rockingham Bay, Cleveland Bay, Rockhampton and Gilbert River.

G. rutæfolia, R. Br. Blanket fern. Rhizome a short knot. Fronds tufted, three to six inches long, pinnate. Pinnæ obliquely obovate or almost fan-shaped, three to six lines long and broad, toothed, lobed, or again somewhat pinnate, contracted into a short petiolule, sprinkled above and more densely covered underneath with brown scaly hairs occasionally glandular. Veins forked and radiating. Sori linear, mostly about the middle of the pinnæ, sometimes almost covering the surface. Very widely distributed throughout the whole of the Australian Colonies and Tasmania.

G. leptophylla, Swartz. Jersey fern. Rhizome a short tuft. Fronds delieate, under six inches high and frequently only two or three inches, the outer ones short with few broadly obovate or fan-shaped segments, often barren, the other erect with a slender black rhachis twice pinnate; segments numerous, oblong or cuneate, two to three lines long, more or less deeply lobed, with usually a single oblong sorus on each lobe, often covering the whole surface. Port Stephens, N. S. Wales; Yarra and Lodden River Vale near Sale, Gippsland, in Victoria; Spring Bay, near the Tamar, Tasmania; Barossa and Lofty Ranges, South Australia; and also in Western Australia.

G. pinnata, F. v. M. Rhizome shortly horizontal. Fronds one to two feet high, simply pinnate, glabrous. Pinnæ three to eleven or reduced to a single terminal one, lanceolate, four to ten inches long, half to one inch broad, contracted at the base into a short petiolule, entire, the prominent costule and rhachis smooth and shining. Veins diverging from the costule, forked and anastomosing. Sori linear or narrow-oblong, very unequal and irregularly scattered. Ranges of Rockingham and Trinity Bays, Queensland.

G. ampla, F. v. M. Rhizome rather thin for the large size of fronds, sealy, creeping like Polypodium scandens up the trunks of trees. Fronds one to three feet long, from simple and entire to deeply pinnatifid, with segments lanceolate and from three to nine inches long, three-quarters to two inches broad, membranous, entire, decurrent and connected by a broad wing to the rhachis, the wing gradually tapering below the lowest pair but continued almost to the base of the stipes. Veins proceeding from the midrib immediately forked, one branch bearing a straight linear sorus extending to the margin frequently but not always, the others prominent, flexuose, with anastomosing branches, and from both are emitted a few short free branches. This fern is nearly allied to, if indeed not really a form of the Indian Grammitis decurrens, Wall. Rockingham and Trinity Bays, and Daintree River.

XXXVI.—ANTROPHYUM, KAULF.

Rhizome shortly creeping. Fronds simple, entire, lanceolate or broad, with longitudinal more or less anastomosing veins, bearing long linear sori without indusium. Name derived from the Greek antron, a cavern, and phyo, to grow. Plants usually found growing on the face of damp rocks.

A reticulatum, Kaulf. Rhizome hairy, shortly creeping. Fronds six inches to one foot long, one to two inches wide, acuminate, tapering to a short stipes, glabrous firm, the veins prominent on the upper surface forming long narrow areoles. Sori all longitudinal, narrow-linear but varying much in number and length. On the damp rocks in the gullies of the ranges of Northern Queensland.

XXXVII.—ACROSTICHUM, LINN.

Rhizome creeping sometimes to a great length or short and erect. Fronds undivided or pinnate, variously veined. Sori confluent, covering the under surface of the fertile frond or pinnæ, which are usually smaller or narrower than the barren ones. Derivation doubtful.

A. conforme, Swaitz. Deer's tongue. Rhizome creeping, scaly. Fronds simple, lanceolate, coriaceous, from a few inches to above one foot long, half to one inch broad, acute or acuminate, tapering into a stipes sometimes narrowly winged almost to the base. Veins parallel, simple or forked, not close, and concealed in the texture of the frond; the fertile fronds are usually smaller and more obtuse. Rockingham Bay, Queensland.

A scandens, J. Sm. Rhizome furrowed, woolly, scaleless, creeping in swamps and climbing up the trunks of trees, and often rooting. Fronds one to three feet long, simply pinnate. Pinnæ of the barren fronds broadly lanceolate, acuminate, rounded or cuneate at the base and shortly petiolulate, three to eight inches long, three-quarter to one and a half inches broad, entire or slightly dentate, coriaceous, smooth and shining. Veins very numerous, fine and closely parallel. Pinnæ of the fertile fronds long and very narrow-linear, sometimes almost terete, sometimes flat and two lines broad. Port Darwin, South Australia, and in most of the coast swamps of tropical Queensland.

A. sorbifolium, Linn. Var. leptocarpum. Rhizome creeping, climbing up the trunks of trees to a great height. Frond pinnate, one to three or more feet long. Pinnæ of the barren fronds lanceolate, acuminate, equally or obliquely tapering into a short petiolule, three to six inches long, four to eight lines broad, often denticulate, smooth and shining but not thick. Veins numerous, parallel, three-quarters to one line apart. Pinnæ of the fertile frond almost filiform, also numerous. One of the most beautiful of climbing ferns, found at Rockingham Bay and Trinity Bay, where some of the large scrub trees have their trunks completely clothed with its long feathery drooping fronds.

A. repandum, Blume. Rhizome creeping. Fronds one to three feet long, the stipes of the fertile fronds generally the longest. Sterile fronds firm, membranous, ovate-oblong, acuminate, pinnate. Pinnæ four to six inches long, about one inch broad, more or less petiolulate, lanceolate, pinnatifid about half way down to the costule with ovate-rotundate lobes, with rather broad sinuses bluntly serrated at the margin and generally bearing subulate setæ in the sinuses ; terminal pinnæ sessile, the base decurrent down the rhachis. Fertile fronds with smaller irregularly lobed pinnæ, the setæ of sinuses more prominent. Veins forming a series of elongated costal areoles, other veins forming a few more square-shaped and smaller areoles, the outer ones free to the margin. Queensland, Rockingham Bay, Daintree River and Cape York Peninsula.

A neglectum, Bail. Rhizome creeping, scaly, dark-colored, hard. Fronds of two kinds, like a Lomaria, one to three feet high, lanceolate in outline, deeply pinnatifid, stipes in the fertile frond more than half its length and bordered by a narrow wing, segments, linear, jointed by the narrow wing of rhachis, but not decurrent, one and a half to three inches long. Stipes of sterile frond half the length of frond, bordered by a toothed or lobed wing to the base. Segments lanceolate, coarsely serrated, teeth almost aculeate, and some again serrate, three to six inches long, half to three-quarters inch broad, joined at the base by the wing of rhachis which is about half an inch broad. Veins as in A. repandum. I met with this beautiful species in a close gully of the Trinity Bay Ranges, in May of 1877. Dr. Prentice tells me that Mr. Hill brought the same species from the North of Queensland several years before, and that he saw while on a visit to England, a specimen of the same, labelled in J. Smith's herbarium as A. repandum, from which it differs widely according to diagnosis given in Hooker's Species Filicum, with which our form of A. repandum perfectly agrees.

A. aureum, Linn. Golden swamp fern. Rhizome, stout, erect, forming immense masses in the salt swamps. Fronds in young plants often consisting of the terminal pinna only ; adult fronds from two to six feet high, pinnate, glabrous, the rhachis firm and smooth. Pinnæ distant, the lower ones petiolulate, the upper often decurrent, coriaceous, entire oblong, three to four inches long, three-quarter to one inch broad, the fertile ones rather smaller and a few only at the upper part of the frond. Veins oblique, very fine and numerous, copiously reticulate ; the whole plant having a yellowish

L

hue. Found in salt swamps, from the Clarence River in N. S. Wales, round the coast to Port Essington in North Australia.

A. spicatum, Linn. Rhizome thick, horizontal, usually found on rocks or trunks of trees as an epiphyte. Fronds simple, four to eighteen inches long, the lowest sterile portion lanceolate or linear-lanceolate, three to nine lines broad the contracted fertile apex linear, several inches long, and one to two lines broad. Veins in the sterile portion obliquely reticulate with a free veinlet within the areoles. Sori in the fertile portion forming a broad continuous line on each side of the costa with the margin recurved over them when young, but at length covering the under surface. Spore-cases often intermixed with peltate scales. Queensland, Herbert River and Brisbane River, scrubs, Enoggera creek ; very plentiful on logs and rocks.

A. pteroides, R. Br. Rhizome short, horizontal. Fronds close and very numerous, pinnate or bi-pinnate, three to six inches long, on a stipes of equal length, very fragile, scaly at the base. Segments linear, three-quarters to one and a half inches long, about a line broad. Sori on numerous, almost parallel veins at a little distance from the costule, so close together as to cover the whole frond except the costule and the margin which is recurved over the sori. At first sight this curious and rare fern might be taken for a form of Pteris ensiformis. Queensland, Endeavour River and Gilbert River.

XXXVIII.—Platycerium, Desv.

Rhizome short and thick. Fronds large, of two forms, the outer ones of each year's growth sterile and horizontally spreading, the fertile ones erect, cuneate, forked or dichotomous, the veins prominent, radiating and reticulate. Sori forming large broad patches in the sinus of first fork, or occupying the ends of the lobes. Name from the Greek platys, broad, and keras, a horn, form of fronds.

P. alcicorne, Desv. Elk's-horn fern. Sterile frond cordate cottony, when young sixteen to eighteen inches, long and broad, rigid, the margin more or less sinuate or obtusely lobed. Fertile fronds attaining two to three feet, contracted into a distinct stipes, dilated upwards, several times forked. Sori or patches of spore-cases occupying the greater part of the ultimate lobes. A stout growth of this species has lately been figured in the Gardener's Chronicle under the name P. Hillii, but with equal propriety many more species could be made out of two Platyceriums. Found on trees and rocks from Illawarra in N. S. Wales, to Endeavour River in Queensland ; varying in form according to situation.

P. grande, J. Sm. Stag's-horn fern. A very large epiphyte. Sterile fronds often two feet in diameter, with very prominent veins, the margins deeply and irregularly lobed. Fertile fronds from a broad rigid winged stipes, expanding to a great breadth dichotomously divided with a very broad truncate sinus at the first fork under which is situated the broad patch of sori, often measuring from six to sixteen inches in diameter. The whole fronds covered with a dense tomentum. Found on scrub trees and often on rocks throughout Queensland; also in New England, the Clarence and Richmond Rivers in N. S. Wales.

ADDENDA.

As the genera Lycopodium, Selaginella, Tmesipteris, and Psilotum, are frequently cultivated with ferns, it has been deemed advisable to add the few Australian species to this work.

Lycopodium, Linn. (The name is derived from the supposed resemblance of the forked stems of some species to the foot of a wolf.) Club mosses. In habit these plants are creeping, prostrate or erect. The leaves vary from thread-like to broad imbricate scales, entire or minutely toothed, and are inserted round the stem usually in four rows. Spore-cases all of one kind, flattened one-celled, two-valved, sessile in the axil of the upper leaves, or of bracts usually smaller or broader than the stem leaves, and forming terminal or lateral spikes. Spores all very small.

L. selago, Linn. Fir club moss. A common European species. Stems procumbent. Branches forked, erect, forming dense level-topped tufts of a few inches high, clothed with dark green lanceolate leaves three or four lines long, point fine. Spikes distinct, but the leaves or bracts similar to the stem leaves. Mountains of Victoria and Tasmania.

L. varium, R. Br. (Plant variable.) Stems stout, erect or pendulous, simple or branched, six to eighteen inches long. Leaves crowded round the stem, lanceolate, sometimes nearly half an inch long, spreading. Spikes terminal, two or three inches long, solitary or two or three together. Bracts leafy, two to three lines long, or small and acuminate. Lord Howe's Island, and mountains of both Victoria and Tasmania. [L. selago, var. F. v. M., Fragm V.]

In the Queensland Acclimatisation Society's bush house at Bowen Park, is a remarkable robust-form of this species. The plant was sent to the Society by a gentleman who gathered it in Northern Queensland, the locality not named. Plant epiphytal, pendulous. Stems dichotomously branched, one and a half to two feet long, without the spikes which are from six to nine inches long, and also forked. Leaves six to nine lines long. This form has quite the habit of L. phlegmaria, but without the marked difference between the leaves and bracts of that species.

L. phlegmaria, Linn. Stems elongated, pendulous, Leaves lanceolate, four to six lines long. Spikes several times forked, six to twelve or more inches long. Bracts closely imbricate in four rows, broad, about as long as spore-cases. This is one of the most graceful epiphytes of Australia. On rocks and trees of tropical Queensland.

L. clavatum, Linn, var. **fastigiatum**. (Referring to the club-shaped inflorescence.) Stems from a creeping base, ascending a few inches. Leaves crowded, linear-lanceolate, about two lines long. Spikes terminal, erect, pedunculate, often a few inches long. Bracts with fine, spreading tips. Moist, boggy places in the mountains of

Victoria and Tasmania. [L. fastigiatum, R. Br., Prod. L. diffusum, Spring. L. clavatum, var. magellanicum, Hook. f. Flora, Tasm.] **L. caroliniana,** Linn. (Carolina, N. Amer., another habitat.) Rhizome slender, brittle, closely prostrate, sending up short, erect stems, the upper part of which is fertile Leaves about two lines long, two rows, often rather longer and more spreading than the other two. Stradbroke and Moreton Islands. Common in Tasmania and Western Australia, where it has been named L. serpentinum, Kunze. in Pl. Preiss. and L. Drummondii, Spring, Monogr.

L. laterale, R. Br. (Referring to the lateral spikes.) Stems erect, but slightly branched, one or two feet high. Leaves lanceolate-subulate, two to three lines long. Spikes few lateral, sessile, half to one inch long. Bracts brown. Stradbroke and Moreton Islands; Blue Mountains and Port Jackson, N. S. Wales, and several localties in Victoria.

L. diffusum, R. Br. (Procumbent and loosely branched.) Plant procumbent, stems branched, shortly ascending. Leaves linear, acute or obtuse, about two lines long, spreading or almost imbricate. Spikes lateral brown, sessile or pedunculate. Grampians, Victoria; and several localities in Tasmania.

L. cernuum, Linn. (Drooping, the spikes.) Stems from a creeping rhizome, two to four feet high, or even more, branching with flexuose forked branches. Leaves spreading, filiform, two to four lines long. Spikes sessile, nodding three or four lines long, often light-colored. Bracts ciliate, imbricate in eight rows, longer than the spore-cases. Upper Victoria River, North Australia; Rockingham Bay, Daintree River, Glasshouse Mountains, Logan River, and other places in Queensland.

L. densum, Labill. (Dense, the branches.) Stems from a creeping base, erect, from one to sometimes three feet high, branched in the upper part. Leaves crowded all round, lanceolate with scarious tips two lines long, leaves of the branches scarcely one line long and imbricate. Spikes terminal, numerous, erect, half to one inch long. Bracts ovate-lanceolate, tips spreading, margins often scarious. Port Jackson, New England, &c., N. S. Wales; Grampians, Mount Cobberas, Upper Yarra River, and Cape Howe, in Victoria; and in many localities in Tasmania.

L. scariosum, Forst. (Alluding to the dry, scarious tips of the bracts.) Stems prostrate, sometimes very long, with short ascending branches. Leaves distichously spreading, decurrent, about two lines long, with appressed ones between the two rows. Spikes terminal, sessile, about half an inch long, with broad spreading bracts in four rows, the tips and margins scarious. Swampy parts of Mount Baw-Baw, the sources of the Yarra, Victoria; Table Mountains, and many boggy localities in Tasmania. [L. decurrens, R. Br., Prod.]

L. volubile, Forst. (Climbing.) Stems slender, very long and flexuose, the leaves of which are narrow and appressed, but on the

numerous leafy branches the leaves are distichous and spreading.
Spikes very numerous at the ends of the branches, about one inch
long. Bracts closely imbricate, without spreading tips. Glenelg
River. A common New Zealand plant, but the specimen from the
above locality was barren, so the Australian habitat is doubtful.
    Selaginella, Spring. (The name is a diminutive of selago).
Differing from Lycopodiums in having two kinds of spore-cases,
small ones filled with minute, powdery spores called *microspores*,
and larger containing one to six larger spores called *macrospores*,
all opening in two to four valves and sessile in the axils of bracts
in terminal spikes.
    S. Preissiana, Spring. (After Dr. Ludovicus Preiss.) An
erect, slender plant of a few inches, divided at the base into simple
forked branches leafy throughout. Leaves all alike, narrow,
spreading, acuminate, about a line long, the greater part of the
plant occupied by the fructification. Bracts in four rows. In the
swamps, Stanthorpe, Queensland ; Fitzroy River, Grampians,
Dandenong Ranges, Gippsland ; Ararat in Victoria ; South Esk
River, Tasmania ; Blackwood and Swan Rivers, Western Australia.
[Lycopodium gracillimum, Kunze in Pl. Preiss.]
    S. uliginosa, Spring. (Plant found in marshy localities.)
Stems from a creeping base, two to twelve inches high, much
branched. Leaves all similar, ovate-lanceolate, keeled, spreading or
reflexed, sometimes oblique, but not vertical. Spikes terminal,
three to twelve lines long. Bracts smaller than the stem-leaves, in
four rows, points but slightly spreading. Stradbroke Island,
Queensland ; and in many localities in N. S. Wales, Victoria and
Tasmania. [Lycopodium uliginosum, Labill.]
    S. flabellata, Spring. (Referring to the flat fan shaped branches.)
Rhizome creeping. Stems erect, very flat, leafy simple, for two to
six inches, then broadly ovate flabelliform for six to ten inches
much more branched. Leaves in four rows, two outer rows distichously spreading nearly vertical, falcate, one to one and a half
lines long, dark green on the upper side, pale and shining beneath,
inner rows not half so long, semicordate, fine pointed, converging
over the rhachis. Spikes three to nine lines long, slender. Bracts
keeled, fine pointed, imbricate in four rows. Rockingham and
Trinity Bays, and Daintree River in Queensland, forming dense
fringes to the margins of streams. [Lycopodium flabellatum,
Linn.]
    S. concinna, Spring. (Name from the neat appearance of
plant.) Stems creeping, slender, pinnately divided, leafy throughout, branches shortly ascending. Larger leaves in two rows,
distichously spreading, oblong, obtuse or acute, one to one and a
half lines long, scarcely cordate at the base ; inner rows smaller,
ovate, appressed. Spikes terminal, four to eight lines long, about
one line diameter. Bracts keeled, acuminate, imbricate in four rows,
the tips usually spreading. Brisbane River, Rockingham Bay,
Daintree River, York Peninsula in Queensland. [Lycopodium
concinnum, Swartz.]

S. Belangeri, Spring. A small compact plant, creeping, but not so intricate as the last, forming patches from one to six inches in diameter. The leaves somewhat smaller and of a deeper brighter green, the latter in two rows, distichously spreading, scarcely one line long, ovate; two inner rows appressed, rather smaller. Spikes terminal, oblong, rarely above six lines long, two broad, the spreading bracts of some very similar to the stem leaves. Port Darwin, in North Australia; and Etheridge River, Rockingham Bay, Trinity Bay and York Peninsula in Queensland. [Lycopodium Belangeri, Bory.]

Tmesipteris, Bernh. (Notched fern. Named from the position of sori, in notch of bract.) Stem simple leafy, the leaves vertical, sessile and decurrent, entire, intermixed with leafy bracts, bipartite on a short petiole, Spore-cases usually two together, united into a capsule-like sorus. Sessile on the petiole of the bracts, transversely oblong, flattened, two-celled and didymous or two-lobed, opening in two valves loculicidally. Spores minute.

T. tannensis, Bernh. (Supposed to have been first found on the Island of Tanna.) Usually a small plant found growing upon trees in the cracks of the bark, the stems seldom more than a few inches in length, but said to attain two feet in Tasmania. Leaves obliquely oblong, about half an inch long or more, truncate or acute at the end, the central nerve produced into a fine point. Bracts replacing the leaves on the upper part of the stem, deeply divided into two segments. Found on trees on the various ranges of Queensland, N. S. Wales, Victoria and Tasmania. [Lycopodium tannense, Spreng. P. truncatum R. Br. Psilotum Forsteri, Endl. Tmesipteris truncata, Desv. T. Forsteri, Endl. T. Billardieri, Endl.

Psilotum, Swartz. (Naked or destitute of leaves.) Stems dichotomus, with distant notches bearing minute scales. Spore-cases usually three together, united in a capsule-like sorus. sessile in the axil of or attached to the bracts, nearly globular, three-lobed, three-celled, opening loculicidally or three valves. Spores minute, uniform.

P. triquetrum, Swartz. (Referring to the three-sided stems.) Found on trees and in the crevices of rocks, at times forming large tufts, usually pendulous. Stems repeatedly dichotomously branched, from a few inches to two or three feet long, three-angled. Scale-like leaves minute and subulate, the bracts subtending the spore-cases, equally small and distant, but forked. Capsule-like sori globular, about one line diameter, attached to the bract below the fork. Common on trees and rocks throughout Queensland and New South Wales.

P. complanatum, Swartz. (Alluding to the branches being flat, not triangular, as in the other species.) Stems flat, dichotomous, pendulous, often three to five feet long, two or three lines broad, rigid or flaccid, the margins alternately notched. Leaves and bracts minute. Capsule as in the last species. Rockingham Bay. [P. flaccidum, Spring.]

REMARKS.

With regard to cultivation, Lycopods differ nowise from ferns: in habit they vary quite as much, some being found on trees and rocks, often in the masses formed by epiphytes; others are met with fringing the margins of mountain streams, and others may often be seen amongst grass on damp hill-sides.

For elegance of appearance they quite equal the ferns, and that they are also appreciated by fern cultivators may be inferred from one meeting with them in fern-houses.

Although their value must be acknowledged more æsthetic than economic, yet we find they have been used in medicine, and as dye producers. The powdery spores also of some species is so highly inflammable that advantage has been taken of this property in pyrotechny.

It may also be further observed that **Lycopodiums** are distinguished from **Selaginellas** by their conifer-like habit, the single form of their capsules. The leaves vary from mere threads to broad scales. The fruit spikes are mostly distinct, cylindrical, and sometime branched. L. clavatum, of which there is a form in Australia, was the badge which was worn by the Sinclairs.

Selaginella may be distinguished from **Lycopodium** by the flat two-ranked stem, and double two or three valved capsule, one of which contains the large pallid spores, the other the free spore-like orange or scarlet *antheridia*, which at length produces the spiral *spermatozoids*. Both sometimes occur together in the axil of the same leaf, but they are sometimes separate. Germination takes place by cellular division of a portion of the spores, and the young plant when produced from the *archegonium* has two opposite like cotyledons, thus resembling the embryo of some exogens.

Psilotum may be recognised from its minute bristle-pointed scale-like leaves, and three-celled capsules.

Tmesipteris, by the large oblong two-lobed capsule, the lobes of which are spreading and acute, and the capsules being situated on the stalk of the bract near where it is forked.

Besides the plants of the order noticed, Isoetes lacustris, Linn, the European Quillwort, and I. Drummondii, A. Br., the Western Australian form. Phylloglossum Drummondii, Kunze, a very small plant, met with in some of the cooler parts of Australia, and the pretty moss-like plants which float on still waters, Azolla pinnata, R. Br. and A. rubra, R. Br. are also Australian plants of Lycopodiaceæ, but are scarcely worthy of cultivation.

Antheridia is a term applied to the male organs in cryptogams, and analogous to anthers.

Archegonium. The long-necked cellular sac, in cryptogams and analogous to pistil.

Spermatozoids. The spiral bodies by which impregnation is accomplished.

A SHORT

GLOSSARY OF TERMS

USED IN DESCRIBING FERNS, WHICH MAY OR MAY NOT BE
EXPLAINED IN OTHER PARTS OF THIS WORK.

Aculeate—furnished with prickles. See Aspidium aculeatum.
acuminate—prolonged into a point. See leaflet of Polypodium
urophyllum.
adnate—grown to or attached lengthwise. See auricles at base of
fronds of Marattia fraxinea.
anastomosing—veins joining like the meshes of a net. See Polypodium irioides.
appressed—pressed close to, as the scales of many ferns.
apex—the summit.
areoles—spaces or meshes of netted veins.
aristate—awned or bearded. See Aspidium aristatum.
articulate—jointed as pinnæ of Aspidium cordifolium.
ascending—applied to the rhizome when it is horizontal with a
somewhat erect apex. See Doodia aspera.
auriculate—having ear-like appendages. See Polypodium subauriculatum, &c.
axil—the angle formed between two parts of rhachis, &c.

Barren—without fructification. See broad lower fronds of Polypo
dium rigidulum.
bidentate—double-toothed.
bifid—*cleft*—half divided or parted.
bipinnate—twice-pinnate.
bullate—studded with bubbles or blisters, as leaflets of Gleichenia
dicarpa.

Capillary—very slender, hair-like.
cartilaginous—gristly.
circinate—curled round like the growing part of most ferns.
ciliate—eyelash-haired.
clavate—club-shaped.
compound—fronds having many divisions.
compressed—flattened.
confluent—running into each other.
cordate—heart shaped. See first fronds of Pteris paradoxa.
coriaceous—hard, tough, like leather. See Pteris paradoxa.
costa—midrib of entire frond.
crenate—regular blunt or rounded teeth. See Pinna of Aspidium
exaltatum.
cuneate—tapering towards the base like a wedge. See pinnules of
Lindsæa microphylla.

M

Deciduous—falling off, as the indusia of Aspidium decompositum.
decompound—having compound divisions.
decurrent—when the base tapers down the stem.
dentate—toothed.   See Asplenium falcatum.
dichotomous—in pairs, or forks.   See veins of Adiantum.   Segments of frond of Schizæa dichotoma.
dimidiate—halved.

Elongated—lengthened.
evanescent—disappearing, as the indusia of some Aspidiums.
exserted—projecting, as the receptacle in many Trichomanes.

Falcate—curved like the blade of a scythe.   See Pteris falcata.
ferruginous—iron-colored, rusty-colored as the scales on rhachis of Dicksonia Youngiæ.
fertile—bearing sori.
filices—ferns.
filiform—thread-like.   See stipes of Schizæa rupestris or Hymenophyllum tunbridgense.
flaccid—feeble.
frond—leaf of a fern.
furcate—forked.

Glabrous—without hairs.
glaucous—a hoary gray.

Hirsute—hairy.   See frond of Polypodium Hillii.
hispid—rough with bristles.

Indusium—the skin covering the sorus in some ferns.
involucre—another name for indusium.

Laciniate—cut or divided.
lamina—blade of leaf or frond.
lanceolate—lance-shaped.   Sometimes applied to general outline.
lunate—shaped like a half moon.

Panicle—branched-fructification.   See Botrychium ternatum.
peltate—stalk fixed in the disk instead of the margin.
petiolule—stalk of leaflet.   See Adiantum.
pinna—leaflet.
pinnate—leaf divided into leaflets.   See Polypodium tenellum.
pinnatifid—leaf divided into lobes from the margin to near the midrib.
pinnule—second pinna or leaflet.
proliferous—when producing young plants upon the frond—as Asplenium attenuatum.
pubescens—downy.   See young fronds of Polypodium rigidulum.

Reniform—kidney-shaped.   See indusium of many Aspidiums.
reticulate—netted.   See leaflets of Polypodium rigidulum.
receptacle—part of vein on which the sorus is seated.

resupinate—turned on its back.
revolute—rolled back. See margin of Cheilanthes fronds.
rhachis—the common stalk upon which the leaflets are inserted.
rhizome—rootstock, or stem of ferns.
rugose—rough, wrinkled.

Scabrous—rough from little asperities. See Dicksonia antarctica.
segment—a lobe of pinnatifid frond. See Polypodinm scandens.
serrate—cut like the teeth of a saw.
serrulate—teeth very fine. See pinna of Blechium serrulatum.
sessile—without stalk, as some leaflets, the oak-leaved fronds of
    Polypodium rigidulum, spore-cases in Marattieæ, &c.
setose—bristly. See Polypodium Hookeri.
simple—not divided, as fronds of Aspleninm nidus.
sinus—recess formed by lobes of the frond. See sorus of Platy-
    cerium grande.
soriferous—bearing the fructification.
sorus—a seed-patch.
spike—See fructifications of Ophioglossum.
spore—seed of fern.
spore-case—case containing spores.
stipes—stalk of fronds.
stoma, Stomium—the opening provided on the side of the spore-
    case, for escapement of spores.
striæ—small streaks. See spore-cases of Schizæa, Pinnules of
    Davallia, elegans, &c.

Ternate—in threes.
tomentose—having close dense downy hair, as Lindsæa lanuginosa.
trichotomous—divided in threes.
truncate—blunt as if cut off.

Umbrosa—growing in shady places, as Pteris umbrosa.
undulate—having a wavy margin.

Verrucosus—warty.
virens—green.

LIST OF AUTHORITIES

FOR GENERIC AND SPECIFIC NAMES.

Abbreviations.   The full name &c.

Agardh.—J. C. Agardh, a Swedish professor and writer on Algæ.

Ait.—W. T. Aiton, a former director of the Royal Gardens, Kew.

Bail.—F. M. Bailey, an Australian Botanist.

Baker.—J. G. Baker, one of the authors of Synopsis Filicum.

Bedd.— — Beddome, a writer on S. Indian ferns.

Bernh.—J. J. Bernhardi, Professor of Botany at Erfurt.

Bl.—C. L. Blume, a Dutch Botanist and traveller in Java.

Bory.—Bory de St. Vincent, a French Botanist and traveller.

Bosch.—V. de Bosch.

Br. or R. Br.—Robert Brown, a British Botanist, author of Pro-
dromus-Floræ Novæ-Hollandiæ.

Brack.—W. D. Brackenridge, Botanist to the U. S. Expl.
Expedition.

Braun.—A. Braun, director of the Berlin Botanic Garden.

Brongn.—A. Brongniart, Professor of Natural History, Paris.

Burmann.—J. Burmann, Professor of Botany at Amsterdam.

Carm.—Capt. D. Carmichael, author Flora of Tristan da Acunha.

Cav.—A. J. Cavanilles, a Spanish Botanist.

Colenso.—The Rev. W. Colenso, a writer on N. Zealand plants.

Colla.—A. Colla, a collector of Chilian plants.

Desv.—N. A. Desvaux, a French Botanist.

Don.—David and George Don, both British Botanists.

Dry.—Jonas Dryander, a Swedish Botanist, librarian to Sir J.
Banks.

Fée.—A. L. A. Fée, a French Botanist.

Forst.—George Forster, a traveller and early writer on Australian
plants.

Gaudich.—A. Gaudichaud, a French Botanist and traveller.

Grev.—Robert Kaye Greville, author of "The Scottish Cryptogamic Flora."

Hoffm.—G. F. Hoffmann, a German Botanist.

Hook.—Sir W. J. Hooker, author of Species Filicum, &c., &c.

Hook. et Arn.—Hooker and Arnot.

Hook. et Bak.—Hooker and Baker, authors of Synopsis Filicum.

Hook. et Grev.—Hooker and Greville, authors of Icones Filicum.

Hook. f.—Sir J. D. Hooker, director of Botanic Gardens, Kew.

Humb. et Bonp.—Humboldt and Bonpland, travellers in America, &c.

Kaulf.—G. Fredrick Kaulfuss, M.D. Professor of Botany at Halle.

Kuhn.— —Kuhn, a German Botanist.

Kunze.—G. Kunze, Professor of Botany at Leipsic.

Linn.—C. Linnè, or, as his name is latinized Linnæus, the great Swedish Naturalist.

Labill.—J. J. Labillardierc, a French Botanist.

Lam.—J. B. de Mannet Lamark, a French Botanist.

L'Herit.—C. L. de Brutelle L'Heritier, a French Botanist.

Linden.—J. J. Linden, a traveller and nurseryman, Brussels.

Luerss.— —Luerss.

Mett.—S. G. Mettenius, Professor of Botany at Leipsic.

Moore, C.—Charles Moore, director of Botanic Gardens, Sydney, N. S. Wales.

Moore, T.—T. Moore, a British Botanist and author of several works on Ferns.

Muell. F. von.—Sir Ferd. von Mueller, Government Botanist, Victoria.

Presl.—Dr. Presl of Prague, a writer on Ferns.

Poir.—J. L. M. Poiret, a French Botanist.

Prentice.—Dr. Prentice, Brisbane, Queensland.

Raddi.—J. Raddi, a writer on Brazilian plants.

Raoul.—M. Raoul, a Botanical writer on N. Zealand plants.

Retz.—A. J. Retzius, Professor of Natural History, London.

Rich.—A. Richard, a French Botanist and writer on plants of N. Zealand.

Roth.—A. W. Roth, a German Botanist.

Schk.— —Schkuhr, a German Botanist.

Schott.—H. Schott, director of the Vienna Botanic Garden.

Sieber.— —Sieber, a Botanical collector.

Sm.—Sir J. E. Smith, founder of the London Linnæan Society.

Sm. J.—J. Smith, late curator of the Kew Botanic Gardens.

Spreng.—K. Sprengel, a German Botanist.

Sw.—O. Swartz, a Swedish Botanist.

Thunb.—C. P. Thunberg, a Swedish Botanist.

Thw.—Mr. Thwaites of Ceylon.

Wall.—Dr. N. Wallich, formerly director of Calcutta Botanic Gardens.

Wickst.—J. J. Wickström.

Willd.—C. L. de Willdenow, a Prussian Botanist.

INDEX

WITH THE SYNONYMS BY WHICH THEY HAVE BEEN
NOTICED IN WORKS ON AUSTRALIAN FERNS.

PAGE.

ACROSTICHUM.
  alcicorne, Sw. Elkshorn. See Platycerium alcicorne, Desv.
  aureum, Linn. Large swamp fern 73
    A. fraxinifolium, R. Br. Prod.
  Brightiæ, F. v M. See A. sorbifolium Linn., var. leptocarpum
  conforme, Sw. Deer's tongue 72
    Elaphoglossum conforme, Schott.
  fraxinifolium, R. Br. See A. aureum, Linn.
  lanuginosum, Desf. See Notholæna vellea, R. Br.
  pteroides, R. Br. Pteris like 74
    Neurosoria pteroides, Metten.
  repandum, Blume. Margin dilated... 73
    Pæcilopteris repanda, Presl.
  scandens, J. Sm. Climbing 72
    Stenochlæna scandens, J. Sm.
  sorbifolium, Linn. Sorbus leaved 72
    Lomariopsis Brightiæ, Bail. Queensland Ferns
  spicatum, Linn. Spike like 74
    Hymenolepis spicata, Presl.
  velleum, Ait. See Notholæna vellea, R. Br.
  virens, Wall. Green.
ADIANTUM.
  æthiopicum Linn. Common Maiden-hair 42
    A. assimile, Sw.
    A. trigonum, Labill.
  affine, Willd. Rock Maiden-hair 42
    A. Cunninghamii, Hook.
  affine, Hook. See A. diaphanum, Br.
  assimile, Sw. See A. æthiopicum, Linn.
  capillus-Veneris, Linn. English Maiden-hair ... 41
  Cunninghamii, Hook. See A. affine, Willd.
  diaphanum, Blume. Transparent 42
    A. affine, Hook.
  formosum, R. Br. Tall scrub Maiden-hair 42
  hispidulum, Sw. Rough Maiden-hair 42
  lunulatum, Burm. Moon-shaped 41
  paradoxum, R. Br. See Pteris paradoxa, Baker
  trigonum, Labill. See A. æthiopicum

ALLANTODIA—from the Greek allas, allantos, a sausage, form
   of sorus.
   australis, R. Br.   See Asplenium umbrosum, J. Sm.
   tenera, R. Br.   See Asplenium australe, Brack.
ALSOPHILA.   Tree Fern.
   australis, R. Br.   Southern   34
      A. Cooperi, Hook. et Baker.
      A. excelsa, R. Br.
   Cooperi, Hook. et Baker.   See A. australis, R. Br.
   excelsa, R. Br.   See A. australis, R. Br.
   Leichhardtiana, F. v. M.   Prickly-tree Fern 34
      A. Macarthurii, Hook.
      A. Moorei, J. Sm.
   Loddigesii, Kunze.   Loddeges's   34
   Macarthurii, Hook.   See A. Leichhardtiana, F. v. M.
   Moorei, J. Sm.   See A. Leichhardtiana, F. v. M.
   Rebeccæ, F. v. M.   Mount Graham Tree Fern   ... 34
   Robertsiana, F. v. M.   Roberts' Tree Fern 35
   Woollsiana, F. v. M.   See A. Leichhardtiana, F. v. M.
ANGIOPTERIS.
   evecta, Hoffm.   Mounted   23
ANTROPHYUM.
   plantagineum, Kaulf.   See A. reticulatum, Kaulf.
   reticulatum, Kaulf.   Netted   72
      A. plantagineum, Kaulf.
      A. semicostatum, Bl.
   semicostatum, Blume.   See A. reticulatum, Kaulf.
ARTHROPTERIS—from arthron a joint, and pteron, a wing,
   jointed pinnæ.
   tenella, J. Sm.   See Polypodium tenellum, Forst
ASPIDIUM.
   aculeatum, Sw.   Prickly 60
      A. proliferum, R. Br.
      Polystichum vestitum, Presl.
   apicale, Baker 62
      Nephrodium apicale, Baker.
   aristatum, Sw.   Awned 61
      Lastrea aristata, T. Moore.
   capense, Willd.   Cape of Good Hope   61
      Polypodium capense, Linn.
      Aspidium coriaceum, Sw.
      Polystichum coriaceum, Schott.
   confluens, Metten.   Confluent   60
      Nephrodium confluens, F. v. M.
      A. melanocaulon, F. v. M.
      Sagenia melanocaulon, Bail.   Queensl. Ferns.
   cordifolium, Sw.   Heart-leaved   58
      Nephrolepis cordifolia, Presl.

ASPIDIUM.—*Continued.*   PAGE.

  Nephrolepis tuberosa, Presl.
  A. tuberosum, Bory.
  coriaceum, Sw. See Aspidium capense, Willd.
  decompositum, Spr.   61
    Nephrodium decompositum, R. Br.
    Lastrea decomposita, Presl.
  exaltatum, Sw. Tall   59
    Nephrodium exaltatum, R. Br.
    Nephrolepis exaltata, Schott.
  extensum, F. v. M. See Aspidium molle, var. truncatum
  hispidum, Sw. Hairy   62
    Nephrodium hispidum, Hook.
    Aspidium setosum, Schkuhr.
  melanocaulon, F. v. M. See Aspidium confluens, Matten
  molle, Sw. Soft   60
    Nephrodium molle, R. Br.
    Polypodium molle, Jacq.
    Nephrodium didymosorum, Bedd. See A. molle, var.
  didymosorus
  obliteratum, Spr. See Aspidium ramosum, Beauv.
  proliferum, R. Br. See Aspidium aculeatum, Sw.
  pteroides, Sw. Pteris like   59
    Nephrodium pteroides, J. Sm.
    Nephrodium terminans, Hook.
  ramosum, Beauv. Branching   59
    Aspidium obliteratum, Spr.
    Nephrodium obliteratum, B. Br.
    Nephrolepis altescandens, Bail. Queensl. Ferns.
    Nephrolepis ramosa, T. Moore.
    Nephrolepis obliterata, Hook.
    Nephrolepis repens, Brack.
    Polypodium ? Beckleri, Hook.
  setosum, Schkuhr. See Aspidium hispidum, Sw.
  tenericaule, Thw. See Polypodium pallidum...
  tenerum, Spr. Tender   61
    Nephrodium tenerum, R. Br.
  truncatum, Gaudich. See Aspidium molle, Sw.
    A. extensum, F. v. M.
    Nephrodium abruptum, Pr.
    Nephrodium truncatum, Pr.
  tuberosum, Bory. See Aspidium cordifolium, Sw.
  uliginosum, Kunze. See Polypodium pallidum, Brack.
  unitum, Sw. United   59
    Nephrodium propinquum, R. Br.
    Nephrodium unitum, R. Br.
ASPLENIUM.
  adiantoides, Raoul. See Asplenium Hookerianum Colenso
  attenuatum, R. Br. Tapering   53

ASPLENIUM—*Continued.* PAGE.
australasicum, Hook. See Asplenium nidus, Linn
australe, Brack. See Asplenium umbrosum var tenera
   Allantodia tenera, R. Br.
Brownii, J. Sm. See Asplenium australe, Brack·
bulbiferum, Forst. Bulbil bearing... 55
   A. laxum, R. Br.
   Cænopteris appendiculata, Labill.
caudatum, Forst. See Asplenium falcatum, Lam.
cuneatum, F. v. M. See Asplenium laserpitiifolium, Lam.
decussatum, Sw. Crossed 57
   Callipteris prolifera, Bory.
difforme, R. Br. See Asplenium obtusatum, Forst.
falcatum, Lam. Sickle-formed 54
   A. caudatum, Forst.
   A. polyodon, Forst.
flabellifolium, Cav. Fan-shaped, spleenwort 53
flaccidum, Forst. Weak-fronded 55
   A. odontites, R. Br.
furcatum, Thunb. Forked 55
   A. præmossum, Sw.
Hookerianum, Colens. Hooker's 54
   A. adiantoides, Raoul.
japonicum, Thunb. Java 56
laserpitiifolium, Lam. Laserpitium leaved 55
   A. cuneatum, F. v. M.
laxum, R. Br. See Asplenium bulbiferum, Forst
lucidum, Forst. See Asplenium obtusatum, Forst
marinum, F. v. M. See Asplenium obtusatum, Forst
maximum, Don. Large 57
   A. speciosum, Baker.
melanochlamys, Hook. Dark scaled 57
nidus, Linn. Bird's nest fern 52
   A. australasicum, Hook.
   Thamnopteris nidus, Presl.
obliquum, Forst. See Asplenium obusatum, Forst
obtusatum, Forst. Obtuse 54
   A. lucidum, Forst.
   A. obliquum, Forst.
odontites, R. Br. See Asplenium flaccidum, Forst
paleaceum, R. Br. Scaly 53
physosorus, Sieb. See Asplenium australe, Brack
polyodon, Forst. See Asplenium falcatum, Lam.
polypodioides, Metten. Polypodium like 57
   Diplasium polypodioides, Metten.
præmorsum, Sw. See Asplenium furcatum
Prenticei, Bail. Prentice's 56
pteridioides, Baker. Pteris like 55
simplicifrons, F. v. M. Simple fronded 52

N

ASPLENIUM—*Continued.*   PAGE.

speciosum, Baker. See Asplenium maximum, Don

sylvaticum, Pr. Wood spleenwort   57

trichomanes, Linn. Maiden-hair spleenwort   53

umbrosum, J. Sm. Shady spleenwort   55

BALANTIUM—from balantion, a pouch or bag, form of indusium

Brownianum, Presl. See Davallia dubia, R. Br.

BLECHNUM—

ambiguum, Kaulf. See Blechnum lavigatum, Cav.

cartilagineum, Sw. Gristly   50

   B. striatum, Sond et Muell.

lævigatum, Cav. Smooth   50

   B. ambiguum, Kaulf.

nitidum, Presl. Shining   50

orientale, Linn. Oriental   50

procerum, Labill. See Lomaria capensis, Willd.

serrulatum, Rich. Small toothed   50

   B. striatum, R. Br.

striatum, R. Br. See Blechnum serrulatum, Rich.

striatum, S. et Muell. See Blechnum cartilagineum, Sw.

BOTRYCHIUM—

australe, R. Br. See Botrychium ternatum, Sw.

lunaria, Sw. Moonwort Fern   20

ternatum, Sw. Grape Fern   20

   B. australe, R. Br.

   B. virginianum, Hook.

virginianum, Hook. See Botrychium ternatum, Sw.

CERATOPTERIS—

thalictroides, Brongn. Meadow-rue leaved water fern ...   24

   Parkeria pteridioides, Hook.

CHEILANTHES—

caudata, R. Br. Tailed   44

contigua, Baker. See Cheilanthes tenuifolia, Sw.

distans, A. Br. Rusty Fern. See Notholæna distans,

R. Br.

fragillima, F. v. M. See Notholæna fragilis, Hook

Preissiana, Kunze. See Cheilanthes tenuifolia, Sw.

profusa, Kunze. See Notholæna distans, R. Br.

Sieberi, Kunze. See Cheilanthes tenuifolia var Sieberi.

tenuifolia, Sw. Curly fern   43

   C. Preissiana, Kunze.

   C. contigua, Baker.

   Pteris nudiuscula, R. Br.

   Pellæa nudiuscula, Hook.

CÆNOPTERIS—from Kainos, new, and pteris, a fern.

appendiculata, Labill. See Asplenium bulbiferum, Forst

CYATHEA—

arachnoidea, Hook. Cobwebby.   32

brevipinna, Baker. Short pinnæ   33

CYATHEA—*Continued.*   PAGE.
 Lindseyana, Hook.   Lindsay's   32
 Macarthurii, F. v. M.   Macarthur's   32
   Hemitelia Macarthurii, F. v. M.
   Cyathea Moorei, Hook et Bak.
 medullaris, Sw.   Black Fern   33
 Moorei, H. et B.   See Cyathea Macarthurii, F. v. M.
CYSTOPTERIS—
 fragilis, Bernh.   Fragile   58
   C. tasmanica, Hook.
 tasmanica, Hook.   See Cystopteris fragilis, Bernh
DAVALLIA—
 brachypoda, Baker.   See Lindsæa cultrata, Sw.
 dubia, R. Br.   Mountain Bracken   37
   Dicksonia dubia, Gaudich.
   Balantium Brownianum, Pr.
 elegans, Sw.   Elegant   37
 flaccida, R Br.   See Davallia speluncæ, Baker
 nephrodioides, F. v. M.   See Deparia nephrodioides,
 Baker.
 pedata, Sm.   Divided like a bird's foot   37
   Humata pedata, J. Sm.
 polypodioides, Don.   See Davallia speluncæ, Baker
 pyxidata, Cav.   Hare's Foot Fern   37
 solida, Sw.   37
 speluncæ, Baker.   Cave or Rock Fern   38
   D. flaccida, R. Br.
   D. polypodioides, Don.
   Microlepia speluncæ, T. Moore.
   Polypodium speluncæ, Linn.
 tripinnata, F. v. M.   Thrice-pinnate   38
DENNSTÆDTIA—
 davallioides, T. Moore.   See Dicksonia davallioides, R. Br.
DEPARIA—
 Macræi, Hook. et Grev.   See Deparia prolifera, Hook.
 nephrodioides, Baker.   Nephrodium like   36
   Davallia nephrodioides, F. v. M.
 prolifera, Hook.   Proliferous   36
DICKSONIA—
 antarctica, Labill.   Woolly Tree Fern ·   35
 davallioides, R. Br.   Davallia like   36
   D. nitidula, Metten.
   Dennstædtia davallioides, T. Moore.
 dubia, Gaudich.   See Davallia dubia, R. Br.
 nitidula, Metten.   See Dicksonia davallioides, R. Br.
 squarrosa, F. v. M.   See Dicksonia Youngiæ, C. Moore.
 Youngiæ, C. Moore.   Young's   35
DICLIDOPTERIS—Inclining two ways, the veins.
 angustissima, Brack.   See Monogramme Junghuhnii,
 Hook

PAGE.

DICTYOGRAMME—from diktyon, a net, and gramme, a line; lines of sori.
pinnata, T. Moore. See Grammitis pinnata, F. v. M.
DICTYOPTERIS—from diktyon, a net; veins netted.
attenuata, Presl. See Polypodium attenuatum, R. Br.
DIPLASIUM—from diplazo, to double; double indusium.
polypodioides, Metten. See Asplenium polypodioides, Metten
DOODIA—
aspera, R. Br. Pickly Fern   51
    Woodwardia aspera, Metten.
blechnoides, A. Cunn. See Doodia a. var., blechnoides
caudata, R. Br. See Doodia a. var. caudata
    D. rupestris, Kaulf.
    Woodwardia caudata, Cav.
media, R. Br. See Doodia a. var. media, R. Br.
rupestris, Kaulf. See Doodia a. var. media
DRYNARIA—from Dryades, nymphs of the woods; or dryinos, of the oak from the form of sessile fronds.
diversifolia, J. Sm. See Polypodium rigidulum, Sw.
quercifolia, J. Sm. See Polypodium quercifolium Linn.
Linnæi, Bail. Queensl. Ferns. See Polypodium quercifolium, Linn.
ELAPHOGLOSSUM—Elaphos, a deer, and glossa, a tongue; form of fronds.
conforme, Schott. See Acrostichum conforme, Sw.
GLEICHENIA—
alpina, R. Br. See Gleichenia dicarpa, R. Br.
circinata, Sw. Parasol Fern   25
    G. microphylla, R. Br.
    G. rupestris, R. Br.
    G. semivestita, Labill.
    G. speluncæ, R. Br.
dicarpa, R. Br. Two fruited   25
    G. alpina, R. Br.
dichotoma, Hook. Forked   26
    G. Hermanni, R. Br.
    Mertensia dichotoma, Willd.
    Polypodium dichotomum, Thunb.
flabellata, R. Br. Fan Fern   26
Hermanni, R. Br. See Gleichenia dichotoma, Hook.
microphylla, R. Br. See Gleichenia circinata, Sw.
platyzoma, F. v. M. See Platyzoma microphyllum, R. Br.
rupestris, R. Br. See Gleichenia circinata, Sw.
semivestita, Labill. See Gleichenia circinata, Sw.
speluncæ, R. Br. See Gleichenia circinata, Sw.
tenera, R. Br. See Gleichenia flabellata, R. Br.

PAGE.

GONIOPHLEBIUM—from gonia, an angle, and phleps, a vein.
    subauriculatum, Presl.   See Polypodium subauriculatum,
    R. Br.
    verrucosum, Bail. Queensl. Ferns. See Polypodium
    verrucosum, Wall.
GONIOPTERIS—from gonia, an angle, and pteris.
    Ghiesbrechtii, Bail. Queensl. Ferns. See Polypodium
    Hillii, Baker.
    Kennedyi, F. v. M. See Polypodium urophyllum, Wall.
    lineata, Bedd. See Polypodium urophyllum, Wall.
    pœcilophlebia, Bail. Queensl. Ferns. See Polypodium
    pæcilophlebium, Hook.
    prolifera, Presl. See Polypodium proliferum, Presl.
    urophylla, Presl. See Polypodium urophyllum, Wall.
GRAMMITIS—
    ampla, F. v. M. Large fronded 71
    australis, R. Br. See Polypodium australe, Metten.
    Billardieri, Willd. See Polypodium australe, Metten.
    blechnoides, Grev. See Polypodium blechnoides, Hook.
    fasciculata, Blume. See Polypodium Hookeri, Brack.
    heterophylla, Labill. See Polypodium grammitidis, R. Br.
    leptophylla, Sw. Slender leaved 71
        Gymnogramme leptophylla, Desv.
    Muelleri, Hook. Mueller's. 71
        Gymnogramme Muelleri, Hook.
    pinnata, F. v. M. Pinnate 71
        Gymnogramme pinnata, Hook.
        Hemionitis elongata, Brack.
        Dictyogramme pinnata, T. Moore.
    Reynoldsii, F. v. M. Reynold's 70
        Notholœna Reynoldsii, F. v. M.
    rutæfolia, R. Br. Rue-leaved 71
        Gymnogramme rutæfolia, Hook.
        Gymnogramme Pozoi, Kunze.
        Gymnogramme subglandulosa, Hook.
        Gymnogramme papaverifolia, Kunze.
GYMNOGRAMME—from gymnos, naked, and gramma, writing;
    appearance of sori.
    Brownei, Kuhn. See Notholæna vellea, R. Br.
    elliptica, Baker. See Grammitis ampla, F. v. M.
    leptophylla, Desv. See Grammitis leptophylla, Sw.
    Muelleri, Hook. See Grammitis Muelleri, Hook.
    papaverifolia, Kunze. See Grammitis rutæfolia, R. Br.
    pinnata, Hook. See Grammitis pinnata, F. v. M.
    Pozoi, Kunze. See Grammittis rutæfolia, R. Br.
    rutæfolia, Hook. See Grammitis rutæfolia, R. Br.
    subglandulosa, Hook. et Grev. See Grammitis rutæfolia,
    R. Br.

PAGE.

HELMINTHOSTACHYS—
zeylanica, Hook. Ceylon. 21
HEMIONITIS—from hemionos, a mule.
elongata, Brack. See Grammitis pinnata, F. v. M.
HEMITELIA—
Godefroyi, Luerss. A doubtful species
Macarthurii, F. v. M. See Cyathea Macarthurii, F. v. M.
Moorei, Baker. C. Moore's 33
HUMATA—The derivation unknown, or perhaps from humatus,
humid, in opposition to Adiantum.
pedata, J. Sm. See Davallia pedata, Sm.
HYDROGLOSSUM—from hydor, water, and glossa, a tongue.
scandens, Presl. See Lygodium reticulatum, Schkuhr.
HYMENOLEPIS—from hymen, a membrane, and lepis, a scale.
spicata, Presl. See Acrostichum spicatum, Linn.
HYMENOPHYLLUM—Film Fern.
crispatum, Wall. See Hymenophyllum javanicum, Spr.
cupressiforme, Labill. See Hymenophyllum tunbridgensi
Sm.
demissum, F. v. M. See Hymenophyllum javanicum, Spr.
flabellatum, Labill. Fan-shaped. 30
H. nitens, R. Br.
flabellatum, R. Br. See Hymenophyllum javanicum, Spr.
Gunnii, Bosch. See Hymenophyllum rarum, R. Br.
javanicum, Spreng. Java 31
H. crispatum, Wall.
H. demissum, F. v. M. Fragm. V.
H. flabellatum, R. Br.
marginatum, Hook. et Grev. Margined 30
minimum, A. Rich. Small 31
Moorei. Baker. See Hymenophyllum pumilium, C. Moore
multifidum, Sw. Much cut. 31
nitens, R. Br. See Hymenophyllum flabellatum, Labill.
pumilum, C. Moore. Small 31
H. Moorei, Baker.
rarum, R. Br. rare 30
H. Gunnii, V. D. Bose.
H. semibivalve, Hook. et Grev.
semibivalve, Hook. et Grev. See Hymenophyllum rarum,
R. Br.
tunbridgense, Sw. 31
H. cupressiforme, Labill.
HYPOLEPIS.
tenuifolia, Bernh. Tender leaved 43
LASTREA—In honor of the zealous botanist, M. Delastre, of
Chatellerant.
aristata, T. Moore. See Aspidium aristatum, Sw.
decomposita, Presl. See Aspidium decompositum, Spr.
flaccida, Bedd. See Polypodium pallidum, Brack.

PAGE.

LINDSÆA—
concinna, J. Sm.   See Lindsæa cultrata, Sw.
cultrata, Sw.   Knife-shaped.   39
  L. concinna, J. Sm.
  Davallia brachypoda, Baker.
dimorpha, Bail.   Queensl. Ferns.   Two-formed   ... 39
  L. heterophylla, Prentice.
ensifolia, Sw.   Sword-shaped   ...   . 4(
  L. lanceolata, Labill.
  L. pentaphylla, Hook.
  Schizoloma ensifolium, J. Sm.
flabellulata, Dry.   Fan-shaped   39
  L. media, R. Br.
  L polymorpha, Hook. et Grev.
  L. tenera, Dry.
Fraseri, Hook.   Fraser's.   40
  Schizoloma Fraseri, J. Sm.   .
heterophylla, Prentice.   See Lindsæa dimorpha, Bail.
incisa, Prentice.   Cut pinnæ   40
lanceolata, Labill.   See Lindsæa cultrata, Sw.
lanuginosa, Wall.   Woolly   41
linearis, Sw.   Linear   39
lobata, Poir.   Lobed   40
media, R. Br.   See Lindsæa flabellulata, Dry.
microphylla, Sw.   Small-leaved   40
pentaphylla, Hook.   See Lindsæa ensifolia, Sw.
polymorpha, Hook. et Grev. See Lindsæa flabellulata, Dry.
tenera, Dry.   See Lindsæa flabellulata, Dry.
trichomanoides, Dry.   Trichomanes like   40
LITOBROCHIA—The origin doubtful, or perhaps from liphos, a
  stone, and brocha, spots; the areoles of veins like
  pavement.
Milneana, Bail.   Queensl. Ferns.   See Pteris marginata,
Bory.
tripartita, Presl.   See Pteris marginata, Bory.
vespertilionis, Presl.   See Pteris inciso, Thumb.
LOMARIA—
alpina, Spreng.   Alpine 48
  Stegania alpina, R. Br.
articulata, F. v. M.   See Lomaria euphlebia, Kunze.
attenuata, Willd.   Tapering   48
auriculata, Baker.   See Lomaria Fullageri, F. v. M.
capensis, Willd.   Pickled Cabbage Fern   49
  Blechnum procerum, Labill.
  Stegania minor, R. Br.
  Stegania procera, R. Br.
discolor, Willd.   Two-colored   48
  Onoclea nuda, Labill.

LOMARIA—*Continued.*   PAGE.
    Stegania falcata, R. Br.
    Stegania nuda, R Br.
    elongata, Blume. See Lomaria Patersoni. Spr.
    euphlebia, Kunze. Well-veined 49
      L. articulata.
    fluviatilis, Spreng. River 49
      Stegania fluviatilis, R. Br
    Fullageri, F. v. M. Fullager 49
      L. auriculata, Baker.
    lanceolata, Spreng. Lance-shaped 48
      Stegania lanceolata, R. Br.
    Patersoni, Spreng. Paterson's 47
      L. elongata, Blume.
      Stegania Patersoni, R. Br.
    procera, Spreng. See Lomaria capensis, Willd.
    vulcanica, Blume. 48
LOMARIOPSIS—named from resembling a Lomaria.
    Brightiæ, F. v. M., in Bail. Queensl. Ferns. See Acros-
tichum sorbifolium L. var. leptocarpum.
LYGODIUM. Snake Fern.
    japonicum, Sw. Japan 22
      L. semibipinnatum, R. Br.
    microphyllum, R. Br. See Lygodium scandens, Sw.
    reticulatum, Schkuhr. Scrub Snake Ferns 21
      Hydroglossum scandens, Presl.
    scandens, Sw. Climbing Snake Fern 21
      L. microphyllum, R. Br.
    semibipinnatum, R. Br. See Lygodium japonicum, Sw.
MARATTIA—
    fraxinea, Sm. Potatoe Fern 24
      M. salicina, Sm.
    salicina, Sm. See Marattia fraxinea, Sw.
MENISCIUM—from meniskos, a crescent; sorus.
    cuspidatum, Blume., was once thought identical with Poly-
podium urophyllum, Wall.
    Kennedyi, F. v. M. See Polypodium urophyllum, Wall.
    proliferum, Hook. See Polypodium proliferum, Pr.
MERTENSIA—In honor of F. C. Mertens.
    dichotoma, Willd. See Gleichenia dichotoma, Hook.
MICROLEPIA—from mikros, small, and lepis, a scale; indusium.
    speluncæ, T. Moore. See Davallia speluncæ, Baker.
MONOGRAMNE.
    Junghuhnii, Hook. Junghuhn's 51
      Diclidopteris angustissima, Brack.
NEPHRODIUM—from nephros, a kidney; form of indusium.
    abruptum, Presl. See Aspidium molle, var. truncatum
    apicale, Baker. See Aspidium apicale, Baker.
    confluens, F. v. M. See Aspidium confluens, Metten.

NEPHRODIUM—*Continued.*   PAGE.
decompositum, R. Br.   See Aspidium decompositum, Spr.
didymosorum, Bedd.   See Aspidium molle, Sw.
exaltatum, R. Br.   See Aspidium exaltatum, Sw.
hispidum, Hook.   See Aspidium hispidum, Sw.
lancilobum, Baker.   See Aspidium decompositum, Spr.
molle, R. Br.   See Aspidium molle, Sw.
obliteratum, R. Br.   See Aspidium ramosum, Beauv.
propinguum, R. Br.   See Aspidium unitum, Sw.
pteroides, J. Sm.   See Aspidium pteroides, Sw.
setigerum, Hook. et Baker.   See Polypodium pallidum, Brack.
tenericaule, Hook.   See Polypodium pallidum, Brack.
tenerum, R. Br.   See Aspidium tenerum, Spr.
terminans, Hook.   See Aspidium pteroides, Sw.
truncatum, Presl.   See Aspidium molle var. truncatum.
unitum, R. Br.   See Aspidium unitum, Sw.
NEPHROLEPIS—from nephros, and lepis ; shape of scale or in-
dusim.
altescandens, Bail.   Queensl. Ferns.   See Aspidium
ramosum, Beauv.
cordifolia, Presl.   See Aspidium cordifolium, Sw.
exaltata, Schott.   See Aspidium exaltatum, Sw.
obliterata, Hook.   See Aspidium ramosum, Beauv.
ramosa, T. Moore.   See Aspidium ramosum, Beauv.
repens, Brack.   See Aspidium ramosum, Beauv.
tuberosa, Presl.   See Aspidium cordifolium, Sw.
NEUROSORIA—from neuron, a nerve, and sorus, the fructification.
pteroides, Metten.   See Acrostichum pteroides, R. Br.
NIPHOBOLUS—from niphobolas, covered with snow; the starry
scales.
acrostichoides, Bedd.   See Polypodium acrostichoides, Forst.
confluens, Bail. Queensl. Ferns. See Polypodium serpens, Forst.
puberulus, Blume.   See Polypodium acrostichoides, Forst.
rupestris, Kaulf.   See Polypodium serpens, Forst.
NOTHOLÆNA—
Brownei, Desv.   See Notholæna vellea, R. Br.
distans, R. Br.   Distant 70
Cheilanthes distans, D. Braun.
fragilis, Hook.   Fragile 70
Cheilanthes fragillima, F. v. M.
lanuginosa, Poir.   See Notholæna vellea, R. Br.
lasiopteris, F. v. M.   See Notholæna vellea, R. Br.
paucijuga, Baker.   See Notholæna pumilis, R. Br.
pumilio, R. Br.   Small 69
N. pancijuga, Baker.
o

NOTHOLÆNA—*Continued.*   PAGE.
Reynoldsii, F. v. M. See Grammitis Reynoldsii, F. v. M.
vellea, R. Br.   Woolly 70
Acrostichum lanuginosum, Desv.
Acrostichum velleum, Ait.
Cheilanthes vellea, F. v. M.
Gymnogramme Brownei, Kuhn.
Notholæna Brownei, Desv.
Notholæna lanuginosa, Poir.
Notholæna lasiopteris, F. v. M.
ONOCLEA—from onos, a vessel, and kleio, to inclose; referring
to sori.
nuda, Labill. See Lomaria discolor, Willd.
OPHIOGLOSSUM—Adder's-tongue.
costatum, R. Br.*
ellipticum, Hook. et Grev.
gramineum, Willd.
lusitanicum, Linn.
parvifolium, Hook. et Grev.
pendulum, Linn. Ribbon Fern   20
reticulatum, Linn. Netted. Perhaps some forms of O.
vulgatum belong to this.
vulgatum, Linn. Common Adder's-tongue 19
OSMUNDA—origin doubtful.
barbara, Thunb. See Todea barbara, T. Moore.
ternata, Thunb. See Botrychium ternatum, Sw.
PARKERIA—In honor of C. S. Parker, who first found the plant
at Essequibo.
pteridioides, Hook.   See Ceratopteris thalictroides,
Brongn.
PELLÆA—from pellos, black; dark color of stipites.
falcata, Fée. See Pteris falcata, R. Br.
geraniifolia, Fée. See Pteris geraniifolia, Raddi.
nitida, Baker. Supposed Cheilanthes caudata, R. Br.
nudiuscula, Hook. See Cheilanthes tenuifolia, var.
paradoxa, Hook. See Pteris paradoxa, Baker.
rotundifolia, Hook. See Pteris falcata, var.
seticaulis, Hook. Pteris falcata, R. Br.
PHYMATODES—alluding to the swelled base of stipes from
phyma, a tumour, or from phymata, tubercles; the im-
pressed sori, giving the appearance of tubercles on the
upper side of frond.
Billardieri, Presl. See Polypodium pustulatum, Forst.
PLATYCERIUM—
alcicorne, Desv. Elk's Horn   74
Acrostichum alcicorne, Sw.
P. Hillii, T. Moore.

* The various forms of O. vulgatum, Linn. found in Australia, might be
referred as representatives of all these species, except O. pendulum, Linn.

PLATYCERIUM—*Continued.*   PAGE.
  grande, J. Sm. Stag's Horn 74
  Hillii, T. Moore. See Platycerium alcicorne, Desv.
PLATYLOMA—from platy's broad, and loma, a margin.
  Brownii, J. Sm. See Pteris paradoxa, Baker.
  falcatum, J. Sm. See Pteris falcata, R. Br.
  rotundifolium, J. Sm. See Pteris falcata, R. Br.
PLATYZOMA—
  microphyllum, R. Br. Braid Fern... 25
    Gleichenia platyzoma, F. v. M.
PLEOPELTIS—from pleos, full, and pelte, a shield; full of scales.
  irioides, T. Moore. See Polypodium irioides, Poir.
  lanceola, Bail. Queensl. Ferns. See Polypodium simplicissimum, F. v. M.
  phymatodes, T. Moore. See Polypodium phymatodes,
Linn.
  pustulata, T. Moore. See Polypodium scandens, Forst.
PŒCILOPTERIS—from poikilos, checkered ; alluding to the veins.
  repanda, Presl. See Acrostichum repandum, Bl.
POLYPODIUM—Polypody.
  acrostichoides, Forst. 66
    Niphobolus acrostichoides, Bedd.
    Niphobolus puberulus, Blume.
  acrostichoides, Sieb. See Polypodium confluens, R. Br.
  angustatum, Hook. See Polypodium confluens, R. Br.
  aspidioides, Bail. Shiny Fern 64
  attenuatum, R. Br. Tapering 66
    Dictyopteris attenuata, Presl.
    P. Brownianum, Spreng.
    P. Brownii, Desv.
  aureum, Linn. Golden. There seems to be great doubts
about this being Australian.
  australe, Metten. Southern 62
    Grammitis australis, R. Br.
    Grammitis Billardieri, Willd.
    Polypodium diminutum, Baker.
  Beckleri, Hook. Dr. Beckler's. See Aspidium ramosum,
Beauv.
  Billardieri, R. Br. See Polypodium pustulatum, Forst.
  blechnoides, Hook. Blechnum-like... 63
    Grammitis blechnoides, Grev.
    Polypodium contiguum, Brack.
  Brownianum. See Polypodium attenuatum, R. Br.
  Brownii, Desv. See Polypodium attenuatum, R. Br.
  capense, Linn. See Aspidium capense, Willd.
  confluens, R. Br. Confluent 66
    P. acrostichoides, Sieb.
    P. glabrum, Metten.
  confluens, Hook. See Polypodium serpens, Forst.

POLYPODIUM—*Continued.*   PAGE.

contiguum, Brack.   See Polypodium blechnoides, Hook.
dichotomum, Thunb.   See Gleichenia dichotoma, Hook.
diminutum, Baker.   See Polypodium australe, Metten.
diversifolium, R. Br.   See Polypodium rigidulum, Sw.
diversifolium, Willd.   See Polypodium pustulatum, Forst.
Gaudichaudii, Blume.   See Polypodium rigidulum, Sw.
glabrum, Metten.   See Polypodium confluens, R. Br.
grammitidis, R. Br.   Grammitis-like   63
  Grammitis heterophylla, Labill.
  Xiphopteris heterophylla, Spreng.
Hillii, Baker.   W. Hill's Polypody   65
  Goniopteris Ghiesbrechtii, Bail.   Queensl. Ferns.
Hookeri, Brack.   Hooker's   63
  P. setigerum, Hook. et Arn.
iridoides, Poir.   Iris-leaved   69
  Pleopeltis irioides, T. Moore.
Kennedyi, F. v. M.   See Polypodium urophyllum, Wall.
lanceola, F. v. M.   See Polypodium simplicissimum,
F. v. M.
Linnæi, Bory.   Queensl. Ferns.   See Polypodium querci-
folium, Linn.
membranifolium, R. Br.   See Polypodium nigrescens, Bl.
molle, Jacq.   See Aspidium molle, Sw.
nigrescens, Blume.   Blackish   67
pallidum, Brack.   64
phymatodes, Linn.   Scented Polypody   67
  Pleopeltis phymatodes, T. Moore.
pœcilophlebium, Hook.   Various veined   66
  Goniopteris pœcilophlébia, Bail.   Queensl. Ferns.
proliferum, Presl.   Proliferous   65
  Goniopteris prolifera, Presl.
  Meniscium proliferum, Hook.
punctatum, Thunb.   Dotted Bracken   64
  P. rugosulum, Labill.
  P. rugulosum, Hook.
pustulatum, Forst.   Blistered   67
  P. scandens, Labill.
  P. Billardieri, R. Br.
  P. diversifolium, Willd.
  Phymatodes Billardieri, Presl.
pustulatum, Schk.   See Polypodium scandens, Forst.
quercifolium, Linn.   Oak-leaved   69
  P. Linnæi, Bory.
  Drynaria, Linnæi, Bail.   Queensl. Ferns.
  Drynaria, quercifolia, J. Sm.
rigidulum, Sw.   Stiff   68
  P. diversifolium, R. Br.
  P. Gaudichaudii, Blume.
  Drynaria diversifolia, J. Sm.

PAGE

POLYPODIUM—*Continued.*
rufescens, Blume. See Polypodium aspidioides, var. tropica.
rugosulum, Labill. See Polypodium punctatum, Thunb.
rugulosum, Hook. See Polypodium punctatum, Thunb.
rupestre, R. Br. See Polypodium serpens, Forst.
scandens, Forst. Climbing 67
   Pleopeltis pustulata, T. Moore.
scandens, Labill. See Polypodium pustulatum, Forst.
serpens, Forst. Tongue Fern 66
   P. confluens, Hook.
   P. rupestre, R. Br.
   Niphobolus confluens, Bail. Queensl. Ferns.
   Niphobolus rupestris, Kaulf.
setigerum, Hook. et Arn. See Polypodium Hookeri, Brack.
simplicissimum, F. v. M. Simple Fronded 67
   P. lanceola, F. v. M.
   Pleopeltis lanceola, Bail. Queensl. Fern.
speluncæ, Linn. See Davallia speluncæ.
subauriculatum, Blume. Eared pinnæ 68
   Goniophlebium subauriculatum, Presl.
tenellum, Forst. Delicate 63
   Arthropteris tenella, J. Sm.
urophyllum, Wall. Tailed pinnæ 65
   Goniopteris Kennedyi, Bail. Queensl. Ferns.
   Goniopteris urophylla, Presl.
   Polypodium Kennedyi, F. v. M.
   Meniscium Kennedyi, F. v. M.
verrucosum, Wall. Warted 68
   Goniophlebium verrucosum, Bedd.
POLYSTICHUM—from Polys, many, and stichos, a row; numerous spore-cases.
coriaceum, Schott. See Aspidium capense, Willd.
vestitum, Presl. See Aspidinm aculeatum, Sw.
PTERIS—Bracken.
aquilina, Linn. Common bracken 46
   P. esculenta, Forst.
arguta, F. v. M. See Pteris tremula, R. Br.
Brownii, Desv. See Pteris geraniifolia, Raddi.
comans, Forst. Bushy bracken 47
   P. Endlicheriana, Agardh.
   P. microptera, Metten.
crenata, Sw. See Pteris ensiformis, Burm.
Endlicheriana, Agardh. See Pteris comans, Forst.
ensiformis, Burm. Sword-shaped 45
   P. crenata, Sw.
esculenta, Forst. See Pteris aquilina, Linn.
falcata, R. Br. Ear Fern 45

PTERIS—*Continued.*   PAGE.
  Pellœa, falcata, Fée.
  Pellœa seticaulis, Hook.
  Platyloma falcatum, J. Sm.
  Feliciennæ, F. v. M. See Pteris marginata, Bory.
  geraniifolia, Raddi. Geranium leaved 44
    P. Brownii, Desv.
    P. pedata, R. Br.
    Pellœa geraniæfolia, Fée.
  incisa, Thunb. Batswing Fern 46
    P. vespertilionis, Labill.
    Litobrochia vespertilionis, Presl.
  longifolia, Linn. Long-leaved 45
  marginata, Bory. Bordered 47
    P. Feliciennæ, F. v. M.
    P. Milneana, Baker.
    P. tripartita, Sw.
    Litobrochia Milneana, Bail. Queensl. Ferns.
    Litobrochia tripartita, Presl.
  microptera, Metten. See Pteris comans, Forst.
  Milneana, Baker. See Pteris marginata, Bory.
  nitida, R. Br. See Cheilanthes caudata, R. Br.
  nudiuscula, R. Br. See Cheilanthes tenuifolia, Sw.
  paradoxa, Baker. Paradoxical 44
    Adiantum paradoxum, R. Br.
    Pellœa paradoxa, Hook.
    Platyloma Brownii, J. Sm.
    Pteris falcata, F v. M.
  pedata, R. Br. See Pteris geraniifolia, Raddi.
  quadriaurita, Retz. Four-eared 46
  rotundifolia, Forst. Round-leaved. See Pteris falcata,
  R. Br.
  tremula, R. Br. Trembling 46
    P. arguta, F. v. M.
  tripartita, Sw. See Pteris marginata, Bory.
  umbrosa, R. Br. Shade-loving 45
  vespertilionis, Labill. See Pteris incisa, Thunb.
SAGENIA—derivation doubtful.
  melanocaulon, Bail. Queensl. Ferns. See Aspidium confluens, Metten.
SCHIZÆA—
  bifida, Sw. Two-cleft 22
    S. fistulosa, R. Br.
  bifida, Hook. f. See Schizæa fistulosa, Labill.
  dichotoma, Sw. Divisions in pairs... 23
  fistulosa, Labill. Pipe-like 22
    S. bifida, Hook. f.
  Forsteri, Spreng. Forster's 23
  rupestris, R. Br. Rock inhabiting... 22

PAGE.

SCHIZOLOMA—from schizo, to cut, and loma, and edge.
    ensifolia, J. Sm.   See Lindsæa ensifolia, Sw.
    Fraseri, J. Sm.   See Lindsæa Fraseri, Hook.
STEGANIA—
    alpina, R. Br.   See Lomaria alpina, Spreng.
    falcata, R. Br.   See Lomaria discolor, Willd.
    fluviatilis, R. Br.   See Lomaria fluviatilis, Spreng.
    lanceolata, R. Br.   See Lomaria lanceolata, Spreng.
    minor, R. Br.   See Lomaria capensis, Willd.
    nuda, R. Br.   See Lomaria discolor, Willd.
    Patersoni, R. Br.   See Lomaria Patersoni, Spreng.
    procera, R. Br.   See Lomaria capensis, Willd.
THAMNOPTERIS—from thamnos, a shrub, and pteris, a fern.
    nidus, Presl.   See Aspenium nidus, Linn.
TODEA—
    africana, Willd
    barbara, T. Moore.   Swamp tree Fern   27
        Osmunda barbara, Thunb.
        Todea africana, Willd.
    Fraseri, Hook. et Grev.   Fraser's 27
    Moorei, Baker.   Moore's...   27
TRICHOMANES—Bristle Fern
    angustatum, Carm.   See Trichomanes candatum, Brack.
    apiifolium, Presl.   Parsley-leaved 29
        T. meifolium, Bory.
        T. polyanthos, Hook.
    calvescens, Bosch.   See Trichomanes digitatum, Sw.
    caudatum, Brach.   Tailed   29
    digitatum, Sw.   Fingered   28
        T. calvescens, Bosch.
        T. lanceum, Bory.
    fæniculaceum, Bory.   See Trichomanes parviflorum, Poir.
    javanicum, Blume.   Java   29
    lanceum, Bory.   See Trichomanes digitatum, Sw.
    meifolium, Bory.   See Trichomanes apiifolium, Bory.
    parviflorum, Poir.   Fennel Fern. 30
        T. faniculaceum, Bory.
    parvulum, Poir.   Small 28
    peltatum, Baker.   Target-like   27
    polyanthos, Hook.   See Trichomanes apiifolium, Presl.
    pyxidiferum, Linn.   29
    rigidum, Sw.   Stiff   29
    tenerum, Sw.   See Trichomanes candatum, Brack.
    venosum, R Br.   Veined   28
    vitiense, Baker.   Viti   28
    yandinense, Bail.   Yandina   28
VITTARIA—
    elongata, Sw.   Grass-leaved Fern 38

PAGE.

WOODWARDIA—In honor of T. J. Woodward, a British
    Botanist.
    aspera, Metten.   See Doodia aspera, R. Br.
    caudata, Cav.   See Doodia var. caudata, R. Br.
    media, Fée.   See Doodia var. media, R. Br.
XIPHOPTERIS—from xyphos, a sword, and pteris a fern shape
    of frond of some species.
    heterophylla, Spreng.   See Polypodium grammitidis,
R. Br.

INDEX TO ADDENDA.

THE CLUB MOSSES.

Azolla, Linn. 80
A. pinnata, R. Br.   80
A. rubra, R. Br.   80
Isoetes, Linn.   80
I. Drummondii, A. Br. 80
I. lacustris, Linn.   80
Lycopodium, Linn.   76
L. Belangeri, Bory.   See Selaginella Belangeri, Spring.
L. caroliniana, Linn.   77
L. cernuum, Linn.   77
L. clavatum, Linn. var. fastigiatum, R. Br. 76
L. clavatum, Linn. var. magellanicum, Hook.   See L.
clavatum, Linn. 77
L. concinnum, Sw.   See Selaginella concinna, Spring.
L. decurrens, R. Br.   See L. scariosum, Forst.
L. densum, Labill.   77
L. diffusum, R. Br.   77
L. diffusum, Spring.   See L. clavatum, L.
L. Drummondii, Spring.   See L. carolinianum, Linn.
L. fastigiatum, R. Br.   See L. clavatum, Linn.
L. flabellatum, Linn.   See Selaginella flabellata, Spring.
L. gracillimum, Kunze.   See Selaginella Preissiana, Spring.
L. laterale, R. Br   77
L. phlegmaria, Linn.   76
L. scariosum, Forst.   77
L. Selago, Linn.   76
L. serpentinum, Kunze.   See L. caroliniannum, Linn.
L. tannense, Spring.   See Tmesipteris tannensis, Bernh.
L. uliginosum, Labill.   See Selaginella uliginosa, Spring.

                                                        PAGE.
L. varium, R. Br.   76
L. volubile, Forst.   77
Phylloglossum, Kunze.
P. Drummondii, Kunze. 80
Psilotum, Sw. 79
P. complanatum, Sw.   79
P. flaccidum, Spring.   See P. complanatum, Sw.
P. Forsteri, Endl.   See Tmesipteris tannensis, Bernh.
P. triquetrum, Sw.   79
P. trucatum, R. Br.   See Tmesipteris tannensis, Bernh.
Selaginella, Spring.   78
S. Belangeri, Spring.   79
S. concinna, Spring.   78
S. flabellata, Spring.   78
S. Preissiana, Spring.   78
S. uliginosa, Spring.   78
Tmesipteris, Benrh.   79
T. Billardieri, Endl.   See T. tennensis, Bernh.
T. Forsteri, Endl.   See T. tannensis, Bernh.
T. tannensis, Brenh.   79
T. truncata, Desv.   See T. tannensis, Bernh.

GORDON AND GOTCH,

Booksellers and Stationers,

QUEEN STREET, BRISBANE.

A large collection of Books on all subjects on sale; which is continually being replenished by fresh supplies, as new works or new editions are brought out. The following list is a selection only from a large number of books on all matters pertaining to the Farm, and the Fruit and Flower Garden.

THE GARDEN AND THE ORCHARD.

	s.	d.
Gardening for Profit; a guide to the successful cultivation of the market and family Garden, by Peter Henderson	9	6
The Flower Garden in Queensland; containing concise and practical instructions on the cultivation of the Flower Garden and the management of pot plants in Australia, by A. J. Hockings ...	1	6
Queensland Garden Manual; containing concise directions for the cultivation of the Garden, Orchard, and Farm in Queensland, by A J. Hockings	3	6
Gardening for Pleasure; a Guide to the Amateur in the Fruit, Vegetable and Flower Garden, &c., by P. Henderson	10	0
Beeton's Book of Garden Management	9	6
Johnsons Gardener's Dictionary with Supplement	8	0
The Flower Garden; by E. S. Delamer	1	3
Familiar Garden Flowers; by F. E. Hulme, F.L.S. F.S.A.,described by S. Hibberd, vols. 1 and 2 each	15	0
The Orchard and Fruit Garden; by E. Watts	1	3
In-door plants and How to grow them by E. A. Maling ...	1	3
Australian Gardener; an epitome of Horticulture &c., by William Adamson	2	6
Gardening for the Million and Amateur's and Cottager's Guide, by George Glenny, F.R.H.S.	1	0
The Fruit Garden; a practical Guide to the planting of Fruit trees, by William Clarson, F.L.S.	1	3

THE FARM AND PLANTATION.

	s.	d.
How to Farm Profitably, by A. Mechi ... ... 6/6 and	2	6
The Farmers' Manual. A Treasury of Information on the Horse, Pony, Mule, Ass, Cow-keeping, Sheep, Pigs, Honey Bee, Poultry, &c., by Martin Doyle	1	3
Small Farms and How they ought to be Managed, by Martin Doyle	1	3
Our Farm of Four Acres, How we managed it, and How it grew into one of Six Acres	2	6
The Farm and Selection, by A. Lincolne	1	3
Mackay's Semi-tropical Agriculturist	10	6
Mackay's Sugar Cane in Queensland	7	6

THE VINEYARD.

	s.	d.
The Grape Culture; Fuller	8	6
American Grape Growing and Wine Making, by George Husmann	10	0

THE APIARY AND POULTRY YARD.

	s.	d.
Handy Book of Bees, by A. Pettigrew	4	6
A Manual of Bee Keeping. by J. Hunter	4	6
Langstroth on the Honey Bee	9	6
Bird Keeping, by C. E. Dyson	4	6
The Poultry Yard, by Miss E. Watts	1	3
Burnham's New Poultry Guide	12	0
The Henwife, by Mrs. Arbuthnott	4	6
Illustrated Book of Poultry, by Lewis Wright	37	6

STANDARD WORKS ON BOTANY.

	s.	d.
Balfour's Elements of Botany	4	6
Balfour's Class Book of Botany	26	0
Paxton's Botanical Dictionary	30	0

STANDARD WORKS ON BOTA

Bentham's Flora Australiensis, 7 vols.		100	0
Brown's Manual of Botany		15	6
First Forms of Vegetation, by Rev. H. Macmillan, L.L.D., F.R.S.E.		7	6
Fragmenta Phytogrophiæ Australiæ contulit Ferdinandus Mueller			
10 vols.		130	0
Maunder's Treasury of Botany, a Popular Dictionary of the Vege-			
table Kingdom, &c., Cloth, 2 vols.		15	0
Calf do.		26	0

FERNS AND WILD FLOWERS.

Familiar Wild Flowers, by F. E. Hulme, F.L.S., F.S.A.	15	6
The Poisonous, Noxious, and Suspected Plants of our fields and		
woods, by Annie Pratt	4	6
Trees and Ferns, by F. G. Heath	4	6
Our Woodland Trees, by F. G. Heath	15	0
The Fern Paradise, by F. G. Heath	15	6
Sylvan Spring, by F. G. Heath	13	0

NEWSPAPERS AND MAGAZINES FOR THE COUNTRY.

YEARLY SUBSCRIPTION RATES.

	TOWN		POSTED.	
The Farmer	34	6	39	0
Field	46	0	50	6
Gardening Chronicle	34	6	39	0
Gardening Magazine	17	6	22	0
Land and Water	46	0	50	6
Live Stock Journal	23	0	27	6
Floral World	9	0	12	0
Florist and Pomologist	16	0	18	0
Sugar Cane	21	0	24	0
American Cultivator and Country Gentleman ...	26	0	30	6
American Agriculturist	12	0	14	0
American Horticulturist	20	0	24	0

MATTHEW RIGBY,

SEEDSMAN

TO

Government House.

ALL PERSONS WANTING

SEEDS OR PLANTS

can obtain, GRATIS, a copy of

→ RIGBY'S BEAUTIFULLY ILLUSTRATED ←

Gardeners' Guide

AND CATALOGUE,

by applying at his Establishment,

QUEEN STREET, BRISBANE,

QUEENSLAND.

www.ingramcontent.com/pod-product-compliance
Lightning Source LLC
Chambersburg PA
CBHW030624270326
41927CB00007B/1300